LAURA AGUILAR

The Tate Photography Series is a celebration of international and British photography in the Tate collection and an introduction to some of the most significant photographers at work today. Previous sets of four in the series have explored the themes of Community and Solidarity, and Ecology and Environment.

Each book focuses on an individual photographer and features a specially selected sequence of photographs, an introduction by a Tate curator and a conversation with, or statement by, the artist. These collaborative books as dialogues between artists and experts aim to enrich our understanding of photography and its connection to everyday life, and collectively they move from city streets to seashores, across landscapes and subcultures, through identities and interiors, in a visual travelogue of our world today.

The theme for Series Three is Queer and Visible, bringing together four artists who use photography to unfold valuable insights into queer life. Each artist uniquely reflects upon societal constructs of sexuality and race, and responds to the experience of living in a predominantly white and heteronormative society.

To see and to make seen, to work in good faith, to produce artful storytelling and resonant images – these are the qualities we seek from good photography. The artist-photographer notices and captures, calls for a moment of our divided and hurried attention, and reveals connection and pattern, emotion and meaning. The work sets out to expand the possible and make hearts and minds more spacious.

Series Three

LAURA AGUILAR

Edited by
Michael Wellen

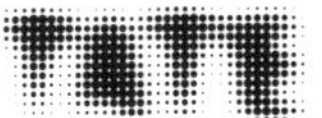

First published 2025 by order of the Tate Trustees
by Tate Publishing, a division of Tate Enterprises Ltd,
Millbank, London SW1P 4RG
www.tate.org.uk/publishing

A catalogue record for this book is available from
the British Library

ISBN 978 1 84976 953 2

Distributed in the United States and Canada
by ABRAMS, New York

Library of Congress Control Number applied for

Series Editor: Simon Armstrong
Senior Editor: Nicola Bion
Production: Bill Jones
Picture Research: Roz Hill
Designed by Sarah Boris
Colour reproduction by Westerham Press, London
Printed and bound in the UK by Westerham Press,
London

Front cover: *Stillness #27* 1999
Back cover top: *Will Work For #4* 1994
Back cover bottom: *Plush Pony #15* 1992

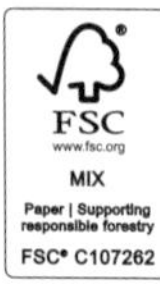

CONTENTS

INTRODUCTION

When you see an image by Laura Aguilar (1959–2018) you're unlikely to forget it. Particularly the photographs she made from the mid-1990s onwards of herself nude in the landscape. Aguilar produced her Nature Self-Portrait series, some of her best-known photographs, in 1996 while on a road trip through New Mexico with fellow photographer Delilah Montoya and in preparation for a show in the UK.[1] In some of the images, her poses draw visual parallels to stones, such as in *Nature Self-Portrait #7*, where her body echoes three boulders in the foreground (p.49). In others, such as *Nature Self-Portrait #5*, she stands with outstretched arms mimicking the branches of a tree (p.54–5).

The impact of Aguilar's artistic work is tied to its nakedness – not specifically the naked body, but the immense feeling of exposure, of laying bare a sense of self. Despite the word 'self-portrait' in the series title, the images are constructed to be much more than portraiture. Part of the power of Aguilar's work comes from the way her images speak to histories of art while constantly bringing into question the politics of representation. The Nature Self-Portrait series channels the formalist beauty of modernist photography in its surprising compositions, and the technical skill in working with light and shadow. But just as considered as those formal concerns are her political ones. In these as well as later photography series Stillness (1999) and Motion (1999), and through performance and video, Aguilar takes common clichés comparing the female body and the landscape, and critically rewrites the visual tropes.

With courage and tenacity, Aguilar made art throughout her life that addressed her sense of alienation, depression and self-doubt as she came up against racism, homophobia, body-shaming, and the social pressures of being a woman in the twentieth century. Her works are the traces of an effort to find her place among diverse interests and intersecting identities. They create an imagery where she and many others have felt their own sense of belonging. She once said, 'Every time the depression comes up, I can look at the artwork and say, "... you feel content there, you feel comfortable there." I'm trying to convince myself I'm not what I always thought of myself: I'm ugly, I'm fat, I'm not worth living ... I am these things, too: I am a kind person, a funny person, a compassionate person. In the photographs I'm beautiful. I'm kind to myself.'[2]

Laura Aguilar was born in 1959 in the San Gabriel Valley, an area bordering the city of Los Angeles and a place she offhandedly referred to as 'the edge of nothingness.'[3] Both her parents were Mexican–American. Her father Paul Aguilar was born in Los Angeles, his parents having resettled from Mexico during the Mexican Revolution (1910–20). The artist's mother Juanita Grisham was of Mexican, American and Irish heritage, but with deep roots to the San Gabriel Valley as five generations of women on her mother's side lived in the region. In other words, they didn't cross the border into the US, but rather the border crossed them when the land that eventually became California was ceded to the US after the Mexican–American War (1846–8).[4] Despite these roots, Aguilar (like the children of many immigrant families in the United States) had questions of belonging. She grew up living in the borderlands – someone who fitted neither into white, heterosexual US society nor into conventionally religious Mexican culture.[5]

In *Three Eagles Flying* 1990, one of the first works she ever exhibited and one of her most iconic, Aguilar symbolically presents herself inextricably caught between two cultures (p.17).[6] We see a central figure flanked by the national flags of the US and Mexico. She is naked and bound by thick rope. The eagle of the Mexican flag covers her entire face, a national symbol turned into a hood that blinds, anonymises and potentially suffocates, while the US flag cinches her waist. The title refers to the national symbols of the two countries and to her last name, which derives from *águila,* the Spanish word for 'eagle'.[7] She comments that the piece 'arose out of the feelings of frustration which derive from my sense of being culturally illegitimate. It represents being tied between two cultures and not being accepted by either.'[8] The work was also one of her earliest to feature herself nude. Independent curator Sybil Venegas, who first included the work in an exhibition at the Laband Gallery in Los Angeles in 1990, comments about the radicality of the image: 'Laura was so far ahead of the times,' she says, 'It was very difficult for many people to visualize the large, brown, female body. It just was something that people did not do. So this in-your-face, powerful image ... it just basically blew her out of the community, and she became known to a much larger audience.'[9]

Aguilar began learning photography in the late 1970s while in high school. At first she took classes so that she could use the camera owned by her older brother John Lee Aguilar, who, seeing her persistence and talent, encouraged her and eventually built a dark room at their home.[10] It became an important creative outlet, away from her parents and the tortures of school, where she struggled with reading and speaking, primarily as result of auditory dyslexia – a condition that was only diagnosed later when she was twenty-six years old.

As a photographer Aguilar considered herself largely self-taught. That said, she readily acknowledged the importance of various teachers and friendships that nurtured her practice. At East Los Angeles College, photographers Suda House, Judy Miranda and Mei Valenzuela were instructors who encouraged and befriended her. Sybil Venegas, then a professor of Chicano Studies, introduced her to key people and places within the city's Latinx art scene. Among them was Self Help Graphics & Art, an artist-run print studio and gathering place that emerged during the Chicano Civil Rights movement in the 1970s; Aguilar photographed their *Día de los Muertos* (Day of the Dead) celebrations from 1984 to 1992. Writer Gil Cuadros, her classmate and close friend, was also an important influence in her life. They motivated each other in their creative work and supported one another as each began to connect with gay and lesbian communities in Los Angeles in the late 1980s. Other close friends included the photographer Willie Middlebrook, who shared materials and advice, and pushed her to print and exhibit works at a bigger scale.

Seeing other photographers working with portraiture, the body and landscape fed her creativity and confidence. Photographer Judy Dater's own nude *Self-Portrait with Stone* 1981 inspired her to begin her Nature Self-Portrait series as homage. She also loved the work of photographer Joyce Tenneson, with whom she maintained correspondence over the years. In one striking letter to her Aguilar writes, 'I think of posibillit.T. ... by seeing you work out there and ... I just keep going'.[12] The letter shows how Aguilar drew inspiration from the photography of others, and recognised the powers that photographic imagery could offer viewers. In the letter she repeatedly speaks about 'posibilit.T'. Her unique spellings here may be intentional or incidental. Either way, it speaks to the ways she frequently experimented with language, evident across much of her early work. It also exemplifies how she transformed difficulties like auditory dyslexia into poetic paths forward.

In the late 1980s and 1990s, Aguilar produced series of works distinctive for their combinations of image and text, and for their sequenced ways of storytelling. Her Latina Lesbians series (1986–90) presents over a dozen photographic testimonies of women Aguilar met through LGBTQ organisations, such as the Gay and Lesbian Community Center and Connexxus Women's Center/Centro de Mujeres, which sponsored the project. These portraits were produced in a period when few positive images of gay and lesbian life circulated in popular culture, and when news media coverage of the AIDS epidemic was stoking homophobia. Rarer still were outlets for sharing experiences and celebrating the viewpoints of lesbians of colour. Latina Lesbians provided both a space for women to vocalise their experiences and to improve representations of gay culture inside and outside of Latinx communities. She says her intention was 'to provide role models, to break negative stereotypes, to develop a bridge of understanding ...'[13] Aguilar made the work at a point when she was beginning to express her own sexual identity openly, and she chose to include herself in the series (p.22). The sitters' statements are each handwritten with varying degrees of bravado, humour and pathos, giving us a sense of the individual, their struggles and states of mind that cannot be expressed in a portrait alone.

Conceived somewhat as a follow-up to Latina Lesbians, Aguilar produced the Plush Pony series in 1992, wanting to photograph the working-class lesbian communities she also identified with. 'This was the counterbalance,' she says, 'I wanted to show the whole community, not just half a community.'[14] These are anonymous portraits of groups taken in the Plush Pony, a lesbian bar in East LA. We see the sitters showing off, having fun, presenting their tough sides and their tenderness towards each other. The bar closed in the early 2000s, so this series is an important record of a queer community in a time and place that may otherwise have been left without a visual record. Devoid of text, these photographs capture a range of group dynamics and candid poses. That dynamism and sense of momentary exuberance makes them ever more precious.

Part of the strength of Aguilar's work stems from her positionality, in that she is not simply an observer but puts herself in a mutual relationship with those she photographs. Art historian Chon A. Noriega observes, 'Aguilar collaborates with subjects who are her peers so that her work is not about power differentials between photographer and subject as is often, if implicitly, the case with … the social documentary tradition itself.'[15] This sense of collaboration underpins the Clothed/Unclothed series (1990–4), which features a range of people from her social circle including people from the LGBTQ community, the Chicanx art community, academics and other professionals in Los Angeles. The sitters posed alone, in couples or in groups, and Aguilar only included those photographs they chose as their favourites. Works in Tate's collection from the series include images of academic and activist Luz Calvo, first in jeans and shirt, and then nude with 'FUCK YOUR GENDER. QUEER NATION' across their genitals (p.32);[16] also images of Willie Middlebrook, both in solo portraits and with his children (pp.31, 34–5). The series effectively uses sequence and our innate curiosity about people's bodies and their private selves. For Aguilar the goal is not just capturing individuals and their different relationships, but making artwork where she says the viewer feels 'as vulnerable as the nude person … because as they view the images, they are hopefully seeing images of themselves.'[17]

Aguilar's self-portraiture series likewise hinge on combinations of vulnerability and visual activism. Will Work For (1993) and Don't Tell Her Art Can't Hurt (1993) use images and text to convey both her commitment to her art and her ambivalence about the art world. The Will Work For series shows Aguilar carrying different cardboard signs, presenting herself as an artist straddling the identities of protester, beggar and struggling labourer as she seeks opportunities to exhibit and find dependable healthcare. In Don't Tell Her Art Can't Hurt, she critically responds to a slogan on her T-shirt that 'Art Can't Hurt You.' Told across four panels with images of escalating tension as she places a gun in her mouth, her narration embraces the power of art while also questioning the injustices and structural power imbalances that constrain artists of colour. These early bodies of work are significant for the ways in which they confront the racism and elitism of both the art market and the museum system, which have prevented access to so many people like her.

Aguilar challenged herself to overcome her own preconceptions and fears in her nude self-portraits. 'It took me ten years to get from starting to doing nudes in the studio to getting outdoors,' she says.[18]

In Sandy's Room 1989 was a key work during this development,
photographed while house-sitting for a friend in Pasadena. She is
seated just below a window and not visible to the outside, but the
artist says she thought of it as 'a challenge. I wasn't standing actually
in the window, but I knew there were people on the other side of that
window.'[19] During the 1990s, she had a breakthrough with the Nature
Self-Portrait series. She continued to explore forms and multiple
meanings of the body in the landscape throughout the decade. In
the Stillness series and the Motion series, both produced in areas
around San Antonio, Texas, she invited other women to be part of her
compositions.

Each of her self-portraits in nature carries a different tenor and
remains open to fluctuating and paradoxical readings. In the visual
connection of her body to large stones, an image may suggest
strength and immutability, but simultaneously conveys a sense
of human vulnerability and the transience of life. The photographs
are uncanny in expressing a connection to nature and fitting into
place, while they also put a large body at their centre that breaks
out of conventional notions of female beauty. Her images are
seemingly quiet and calm scenes, but they connect the artist
and her collaborators to a landscape that has endured long histories
of colonisation and conflict.[20] In their mystery and queerness, there's
an opening to rethink bodies and places anew – an unforgettable
sense of possibility.

Michael Wellen
Senior Curator, International Art, Tate Modern

1   The Nature Self-Portrait series was commissioned and first shown
    in the UK for the two-person show *Shifting Terrains: Laura Aguilar
    & Maxine Walker* at Zone Gallery in Newcastle upon Tyne, 6 March–
    22 April 1997.
2   This comment by the artist comes from the documentary *Laura
    Aguilar: Life, The Body, Her Perspective* (2009) directed by Michael
    Stone. It is referenced in Marco Antonio Flores, 'Laura Aguilar:
    Transformative Visual Acts in Chicanx and Latinx Portraiture', *Medium*,
    21 Sept. 2020. https://medium.com/center-for-comparative-studies-
    in-race-and/laura-aguilar-transformative-visual-acts-in-chicanx-and-
    latinx-portraiture-6ca08eeb038 [accessed 24 July 2024].
3   Aguilar described where she's from in this way to Sybil Venegas.
    See Sybil Venegas, 'Take Me to the River: The Photography of Laura
    Aguilar' in *Laura Aguilar: Show and Tell,* exh. cat., Vincent Price Art
    Museum, eds. Rebecca Epstein and Sybil Venegas, Los Angeles 2017.
4   For a fuller family history see Venegas's essay in the catalogue cited
    above.
5   Chicana poet, activist and educator Gloria Anzaldúa famously
    theorised the notion of the borderland. She writes, 'Living on borders
    and in margins, keeping intact one's shifting and multiple identity and
    integrity, is like trying to swim in a new element, an "alien" element …
    And yes, the "alien" element has become familiar—never comfortable,
    not with society's clamor to uphold the old, to rejoin the flock, to go
    with the herd. No, not comfortable but home.' See Gloria Anzaldúa,
    Borderlands/La Frontera: The New Mestiza, 4th edition 2012, p.19.
6   *Three Eagles Flying* and the series *How Mexican is Mexican* were
    featured in the exhibition *Image and Identity: Recent Chicana Art
    from 'La Reina del Pueblo de Los Angeles de la Porcincula'*, curated
    by Sybil Venegas at the Loyola Marymount University's Laband Art
    Gallery in 1990. Aguilar cites this exhibition as having been crucial for
    herself and for others to recognise her as an artist and not only what
    she referred to as a 'PR photographer.' See Laura Aguilar, interview
    with Carolina A. Miranda, 14 and 15 May 2018, Los Angeles, California.
    CSRC Oral Histories Series, Los Angeles 2018, no.17, p.63. https://www.
    chicano.ucla.edu/files/OHS_Aguilar.pdf [accessed 25 July 2024].
7   Ibid.
8   Laura Aguilar's statement appears on the website created by her trust:
    https://www.lauraaguilarphotography.com/works/threeeaglesflying
    [accessed 25 July 2024]
9   Quoted in Kerry Cardoza, 'How Photographer Laura Aguilar Uplifted
    Queer, Chicano Identities', *Chicago Magazine*, 28 March 2019.
    Available online at https://www.chicano.ucla.edu/files/news/How%20
    Photographer%20Laura%20Aguilar%20Uplifted%20Queer%20
    032819.pdf [accessed 25 July 2024].
10 See Laura Aguilar, interview with Carolina A. Miranda, 14 and 15 May
    2018, Los Angeles, California. *CSRC Oral Histories Series*, Los Angeles
    2018, no.17, pp.24–5. https://www.chicano.ucla.edu/files/OHS_Aguilar.
    pdf [accessed 25 July 2024].
11 Various well-known artists across the Latinx community have
    participated in the Día de los Muertos activities since they first
    began at Self Help Graphics & Art in 1973. Among them are members
    of the art groups Asco – founded by Harry Gamboa, Jr., Gronk,
    Willie Herron III and Patssi Valdez – and artists such as Carlos
    Almaraz, Judy Baca and Ester Hernandez, and the collective Los
    Four. See *Self Help Graphics at Fifty: A Cornerstone of Latinx Art
    and Collaborative Artmaking*, eds. Tatiana Reinoza and Karen Mary
    Davalos, Oakland 2023.
12 Laura Aguilar, personal letter to Joyce Tenneson, 7 September 1991,
    located in the Department of Special Collections, Stanford University
    Libraries and reproduced in Yxta Maya Murray, 'Laura Aguilar Was a
    Proud Latina Lesbian, and She Flaunted It', *Aperture*, 12 November
    2019, https://aperture.org/editorial/laura-aguilar-yxta-maya-murray/
    [accessed 25 July 2024].
13 Laura Aguilar's statement appears on the website created by her trust:
    https://www.lauraaguilarphotography.com/works/latinalesbians-jc7sz
    [accessed 25 July 2024].

14 Laura Aguilar quoted in Carolina A. Miranda, 'Stories of the Plush Pony: Artist Laura Aguilar's portraits capture a lost era at a working-class lesbian bar,' *Los Angeles Times*, 3 Nov. 2017. https://www.latimes.com/entertainment/arts/miranda/la-et-cam-plush-pony-laura-aguilar-vpam-20171102-htmlstory.html [accessed 25 July 2024].

15 Chon A. Noriega, 'Laura Aguilar: Clothed Unclothed: Challenging Normative Conceptions of the Body', *CSW Update* (UCLA Center for the Study of Women), May 2008, p.1. https://escholarship.org/content/qt0vw2z527/qt0vw2z527_noSplash_e5cde0225960d8ba8b4e52647438e7c4.pdf?t=li4kez [accessed 25 July 2024].

16 Queer Nation is an activist organisation founded in 1990 and known for its confrontational tactics and use of slogans to give visibility to people identifying as queer.

17 This comment from the documentary *Laura Aguilar: Life, The Body, Her Perspective* is quoted in Liz Ordway, 'The Power of Fat Liberation: Rereading Laura Aguilar's Nude Self Portraits', *Sightlines* 2022, p.59. https://static1.squarespace.com/static/5d546015fb293c0001f7ae73/t/635197950cc06427eeeaecba/1666291606987/VCS_Sightlines_Interior_2022_Ordway_Liz_Pages.pdf [accessed 25 July 2024].

18 Laura Aguilar, interview with Carolina A. Miranda, 14 and 15 May 2018, Los Angeles, California. *CSRC Oral Histories Series*, Los Angeles 2018, no.17, p.186.

19 Ibid., p 79.

20 For a further reading of the decolonial aspects of Aguilar's images, see Macarena Gómez-Barris, 'Mestiza Cultural Memory: The Self-Ecologies of Laura Aguilar' in *Laura Aguilar: Show and Tell,* exh. cat., Vincent Price Art Museum, eds. Rebecca Epstein and Sybil Venegas, Los Angeles 2017.

ARTIST STATEMENT
C.1999

I am a visual artist who primarily works in photography, although I have tip-toed into video and performance. I have also been engaged in public service through the work that I have done with at-risk youth through the juvenile correctional system at the California Youth Authority, among others. I like the image of tip-toeing through my discipline because it implies that I am willing to explore different themes, approaches and ideas that I have not previously explored. Since 1985 I have been exhibiting my photographic artwork locally, nationally and now, internationally.

As you can see from the body of work that I have submitted, my journey as an artist is both personal and political because I highlight the sociological by showing a world composed of individuals (myself included as subject) who are varied, assertive and intimate. I have concentrated on identity, culture and outsider status, which mostly means that my work reflects people of color, gender and size. A lot of my past work was concerned with the body – my own and others. As you can tell from my work, I have an interest in how large vessels move within increasingly compact societies, both physically and intellectually.

Over the last few years I have begun to experiment, through photographic art, with how the body moves. This has also led me to begin investigating the spiritual aspects of the body and how it rejuvenates through nature. I am in search of images that can convey balance, grace and serenity. This is obviously a shift in my own perceptions and desires, moving from Urban Portraiture to a larger idea of seeing ourselves in the ever expanding and shifting relationship to nature. In a way I was always moving towards a culture, but now the definition of what it is has been profoundly shifted for me.

I was always defined by (and proudly accepted) the identity markers that were given to me; Chicana, female, lesbian, working-class, etc. But, now I am expanding those ideas to include a larger world view that positions me as central to the landscape of nature. Maybe this has to do more with the idea that as a working artist and woman, I am always stuck between a rock and a hard place!

These images have also served as a form of empowerment and acceptance for the audience and myself. Women taking ownership of their bodies and allowing forgiveness of self as a form of healing is one of the ways in which I have approached my work. It is as much a formal experiment as it is a societal gift.

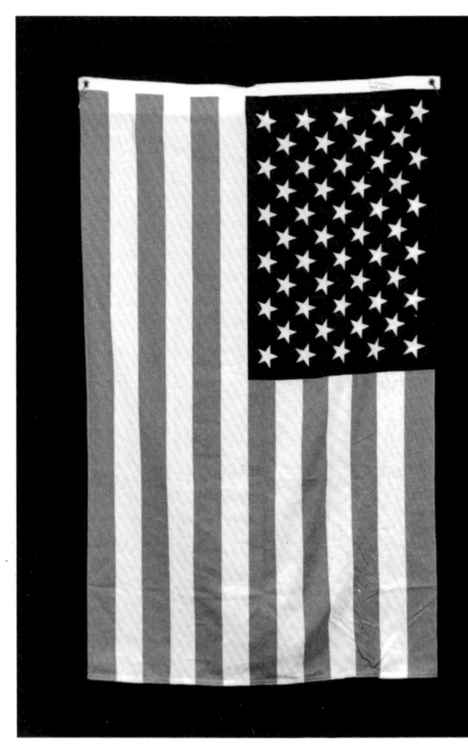

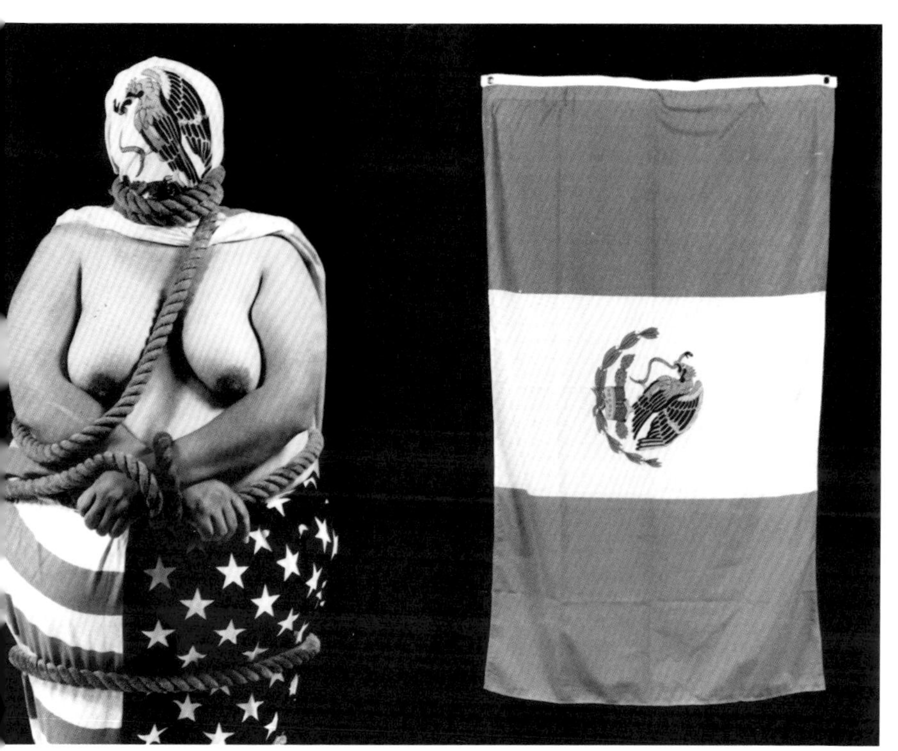

    Three Eagles Flying 1990

LATINA LESBIANS

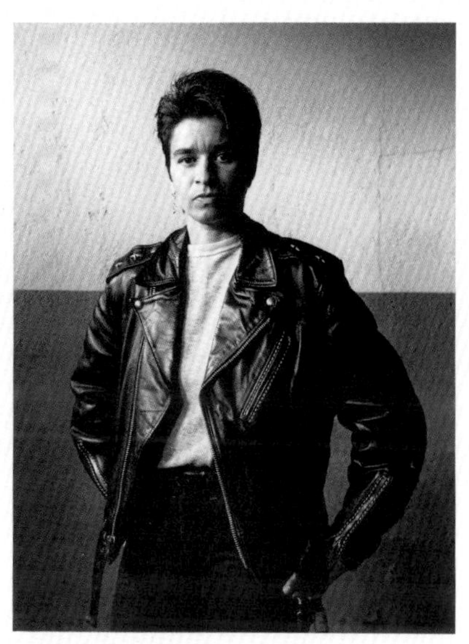

My mother encouraged me to be a
court reporter...
I became a lawyer

Carla Barboza Esq.

    Carla Barboza from the Latina Lesbians series 1987

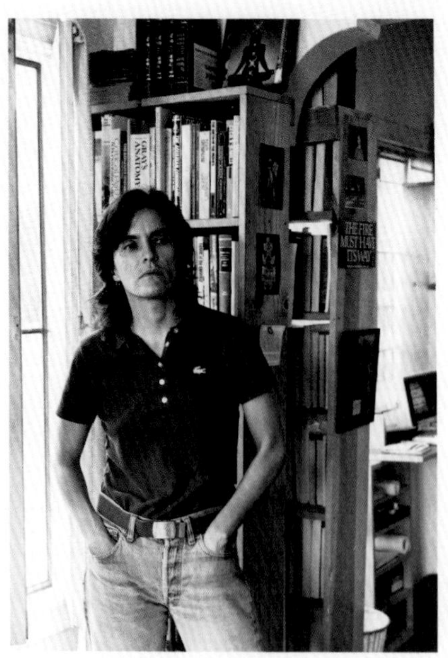

My latina side infuses my lesbian side with chispa
& pasión. I am a lifelong lesbian and I think that
women hold powerful promise for changing conditions
on the planet. You think I look hostile? Maybe
it has to do with a passion for and an impatience
with a vision. Maybe it comes from comparing
what could be with what is. ¡! y qué?!

    Yolanda from the Latina Lesbians series 1987

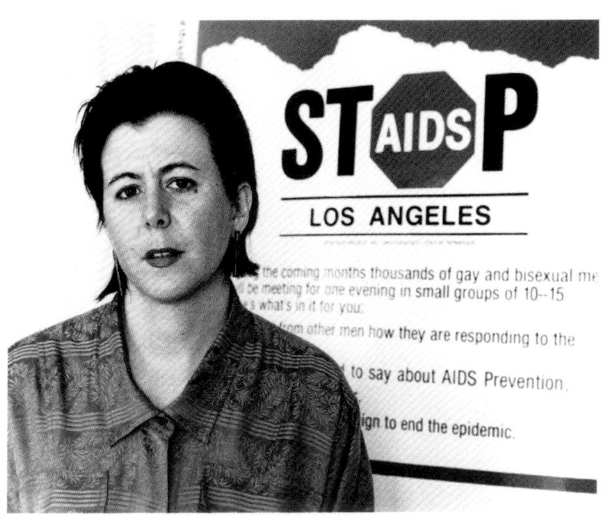

Most of my life I have been a "professional
lesbian." I have worked with gay and lesbian
issues, including AIDS for the last nine years.
I feel we should work together for
equal protection under the law and that
we should accept the increasing diversity
in our community.

     Julia from the Latina Lesbians series 1990

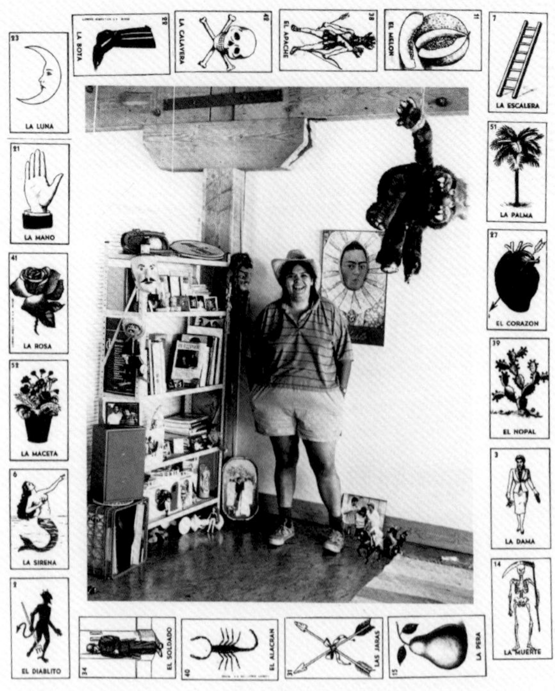

Im not comfortable with the word
Lesbian but as each day go's by I'm
more and more comfortable with the
word LAURA. I know some people
see me as very child like, naive.
Maybe so. I am. But I will be
damned if I let this part
of me die!

   Laura from the Latina Lesbians series 1988

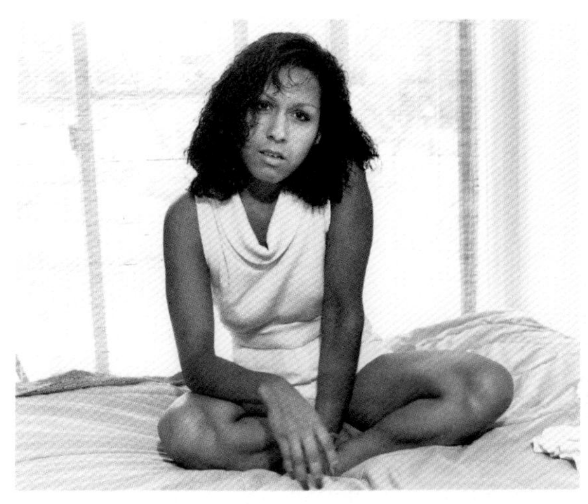

I missed the help of my mother, to find my socks or even to brush my hair. The first time I noticed rain, I ran to school, I arrived soaked, my teacher asked me why didn't my mother cover me properly; I just sat there and cried as I took off my wet socks.

 Angie from the Latina Lesbians series 1988

PLUSH PONY

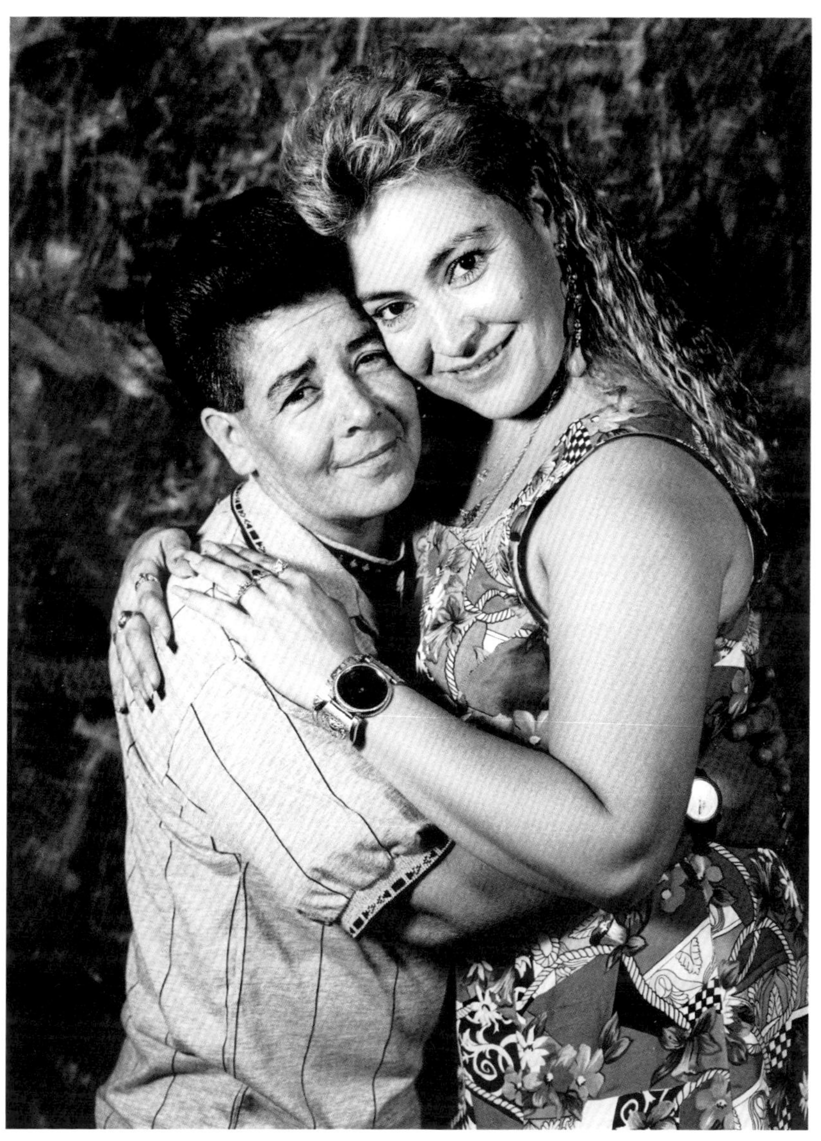

    Plush Pony #15 1992

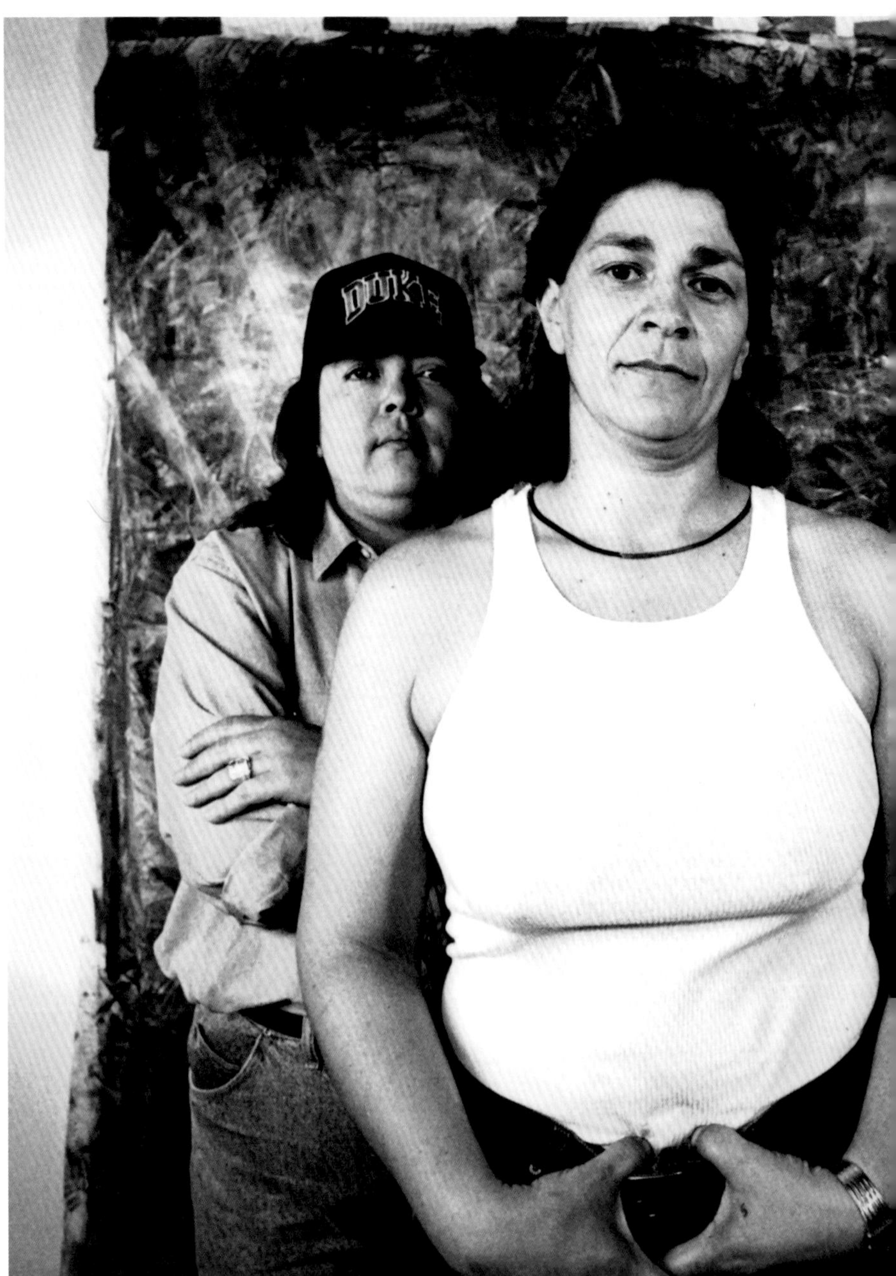

     Plush Pony #2 1992

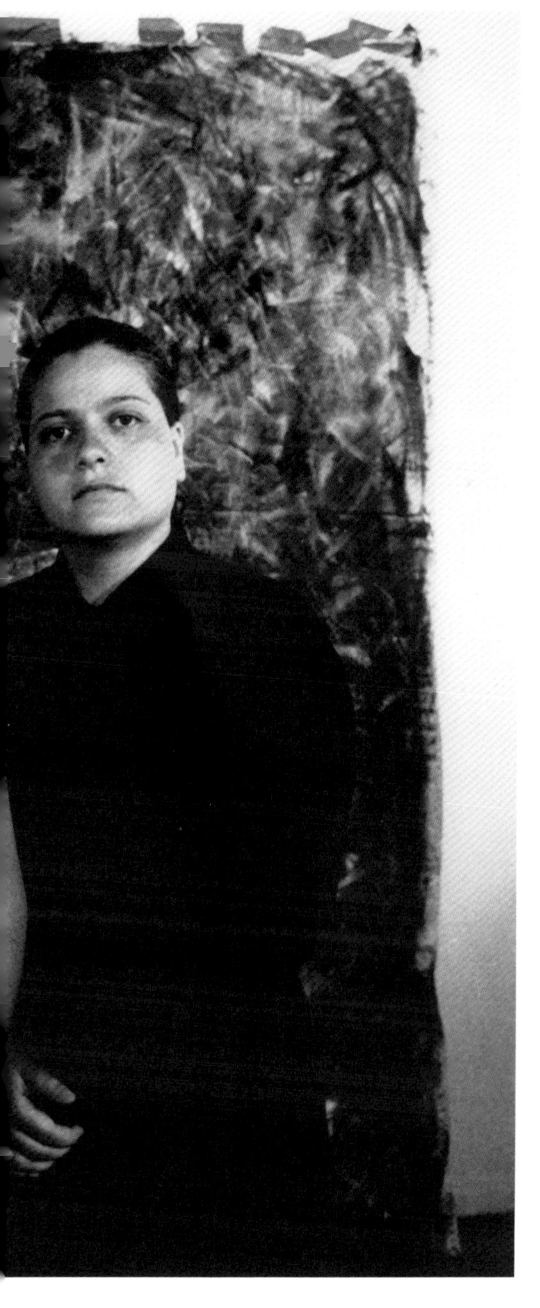

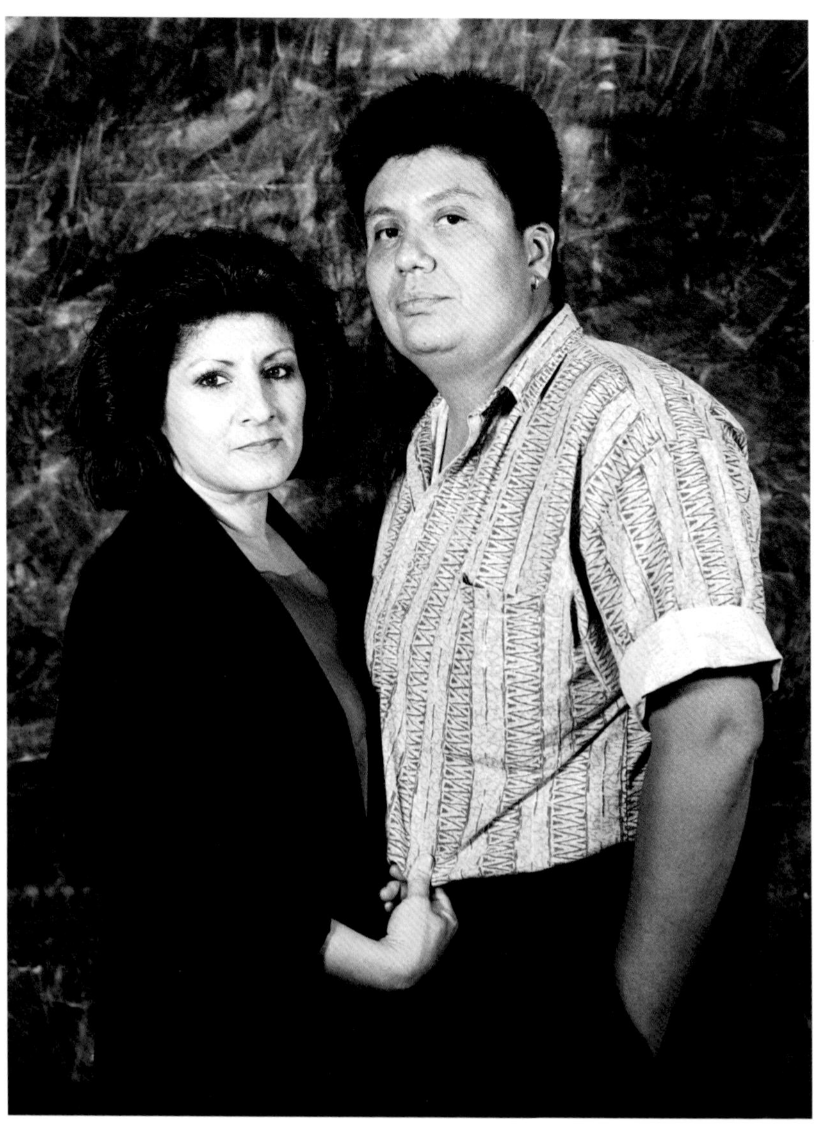

        Plush Pony #12 1992

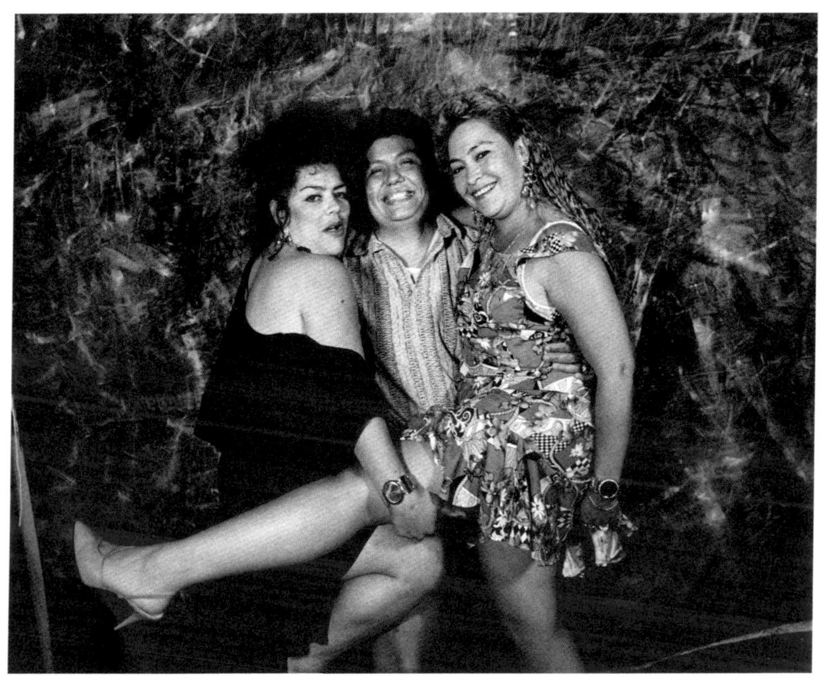

     Plush Pony #7 1992

CLOTHED / UNCLOTHED

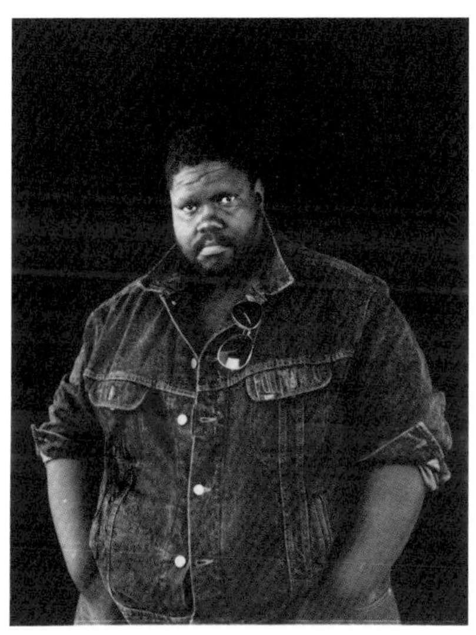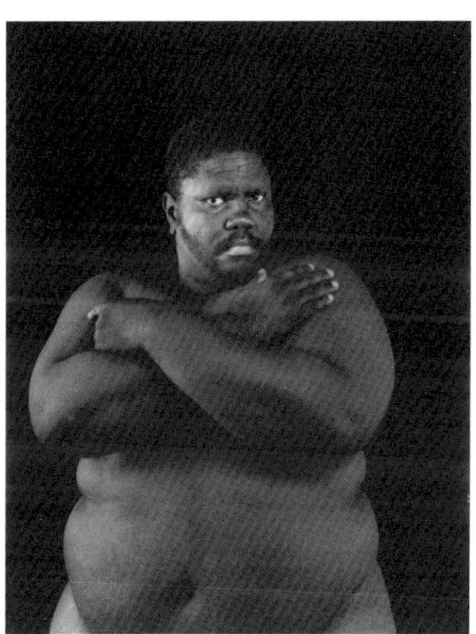

   Clothed/Unclothed #4 1990

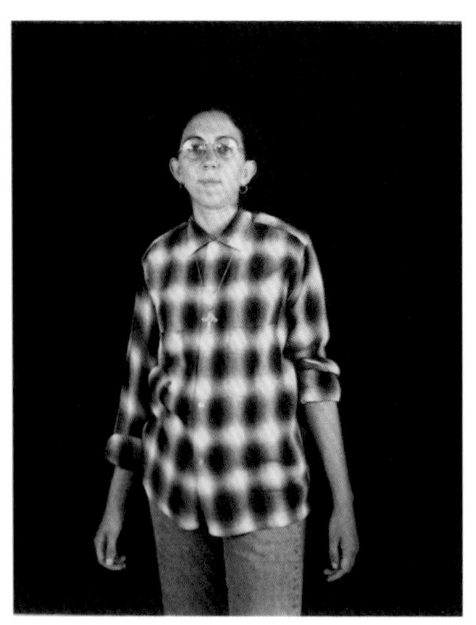 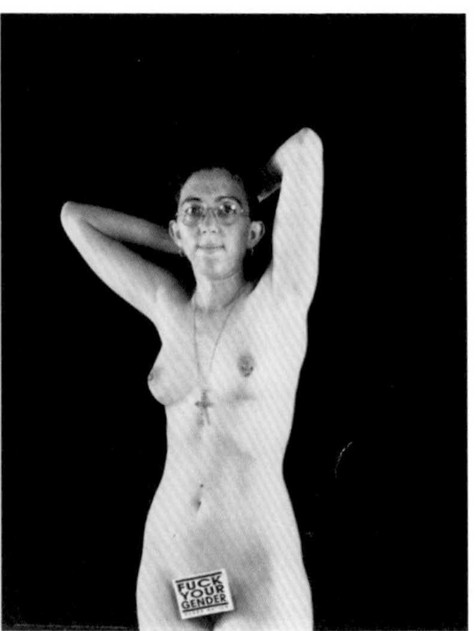

   Clothed/Unclothed #14 1991

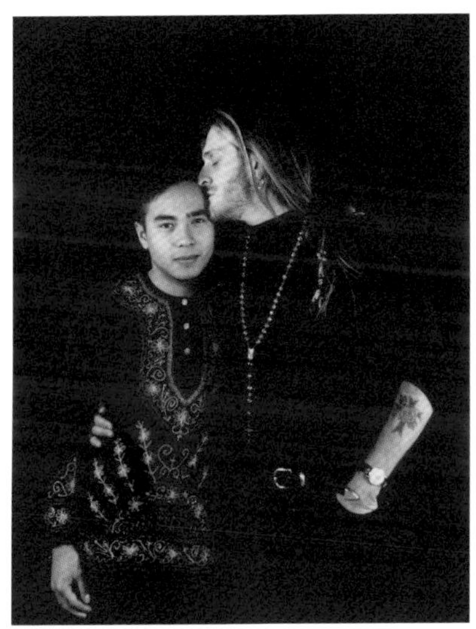 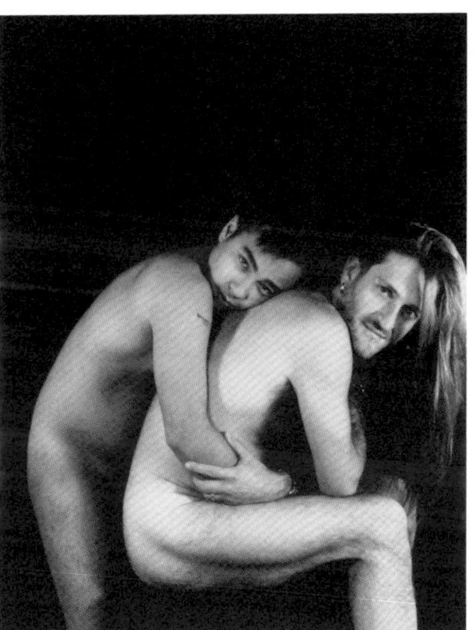

    Clothed/Unclothed #24 1991

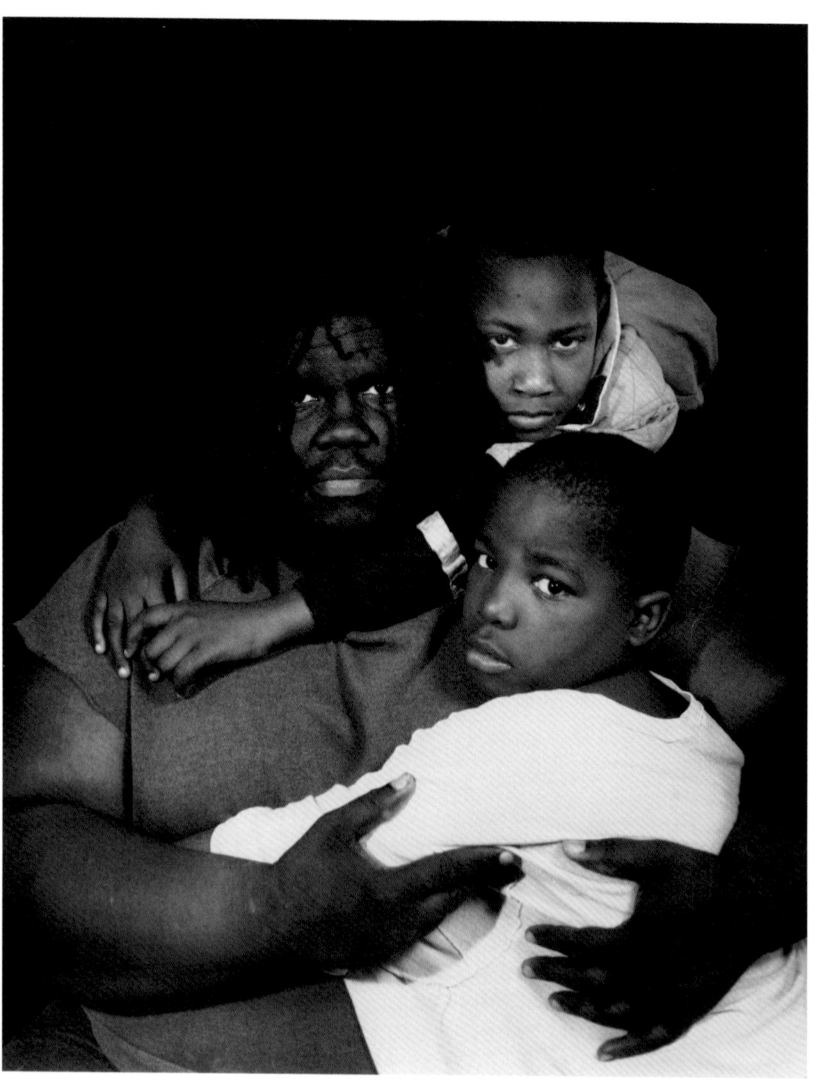

          Clothed/Unclothed #34 1994

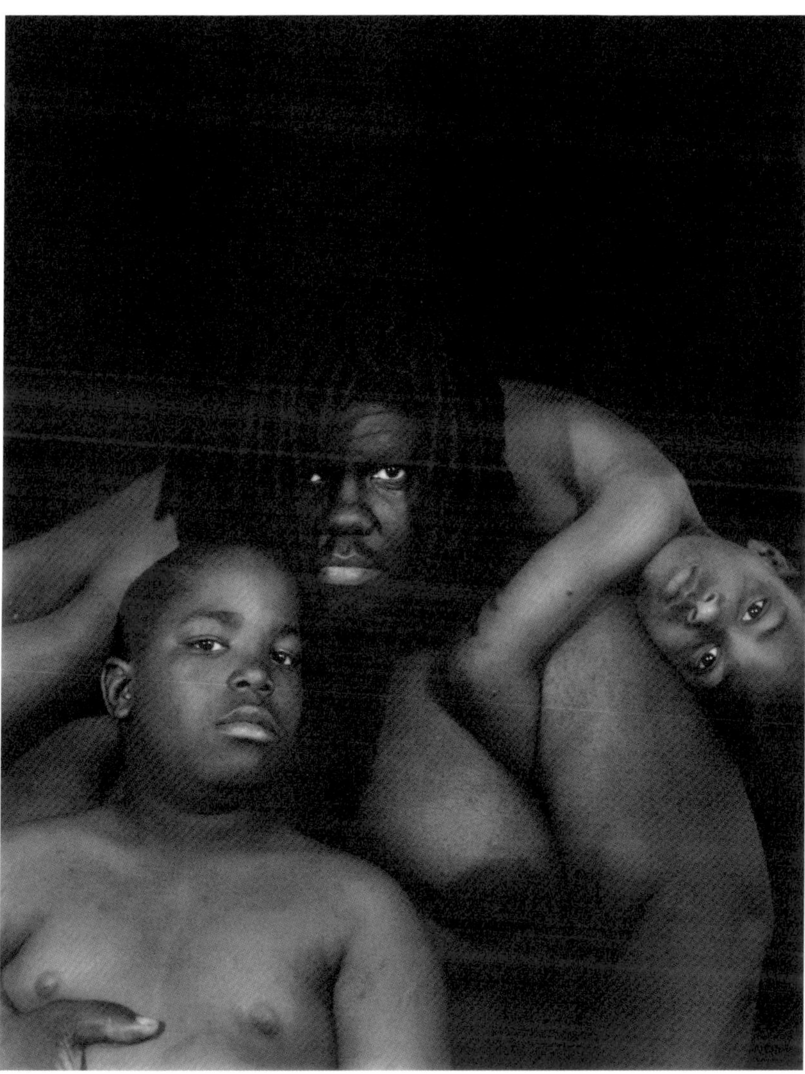

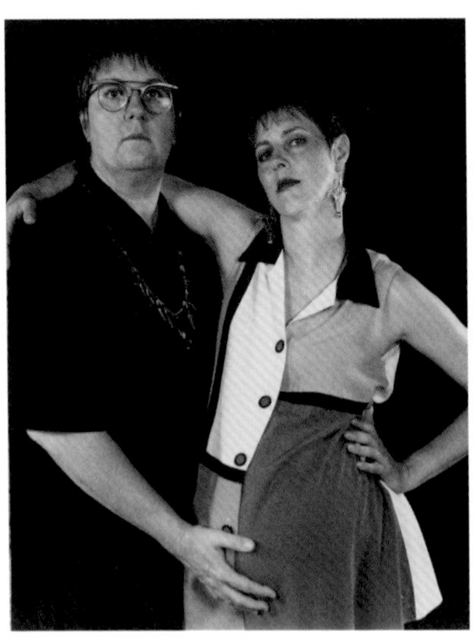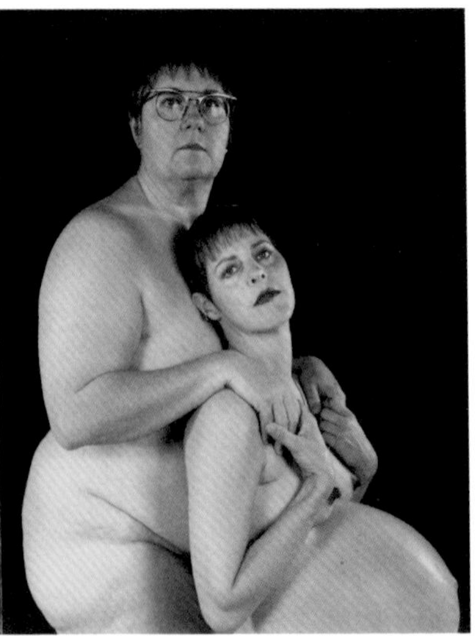

 Clothed/Unclothed #30 1994

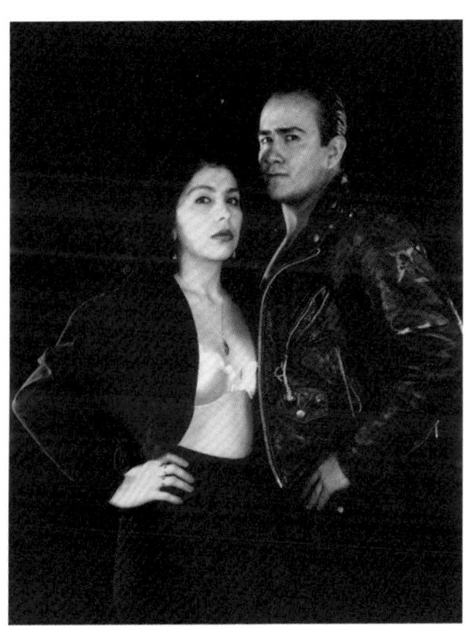 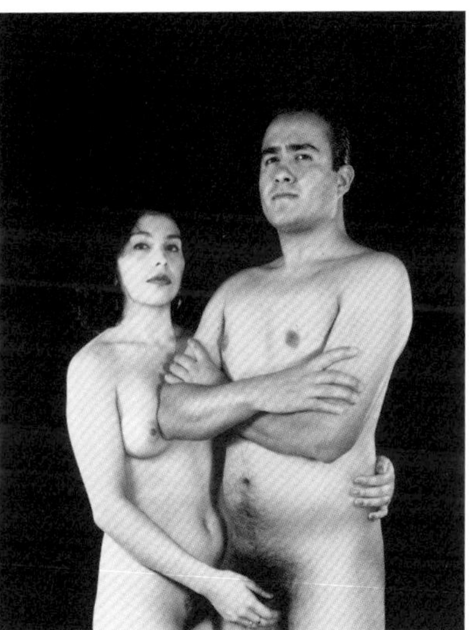

   Clothed/Unclothed #28 1994

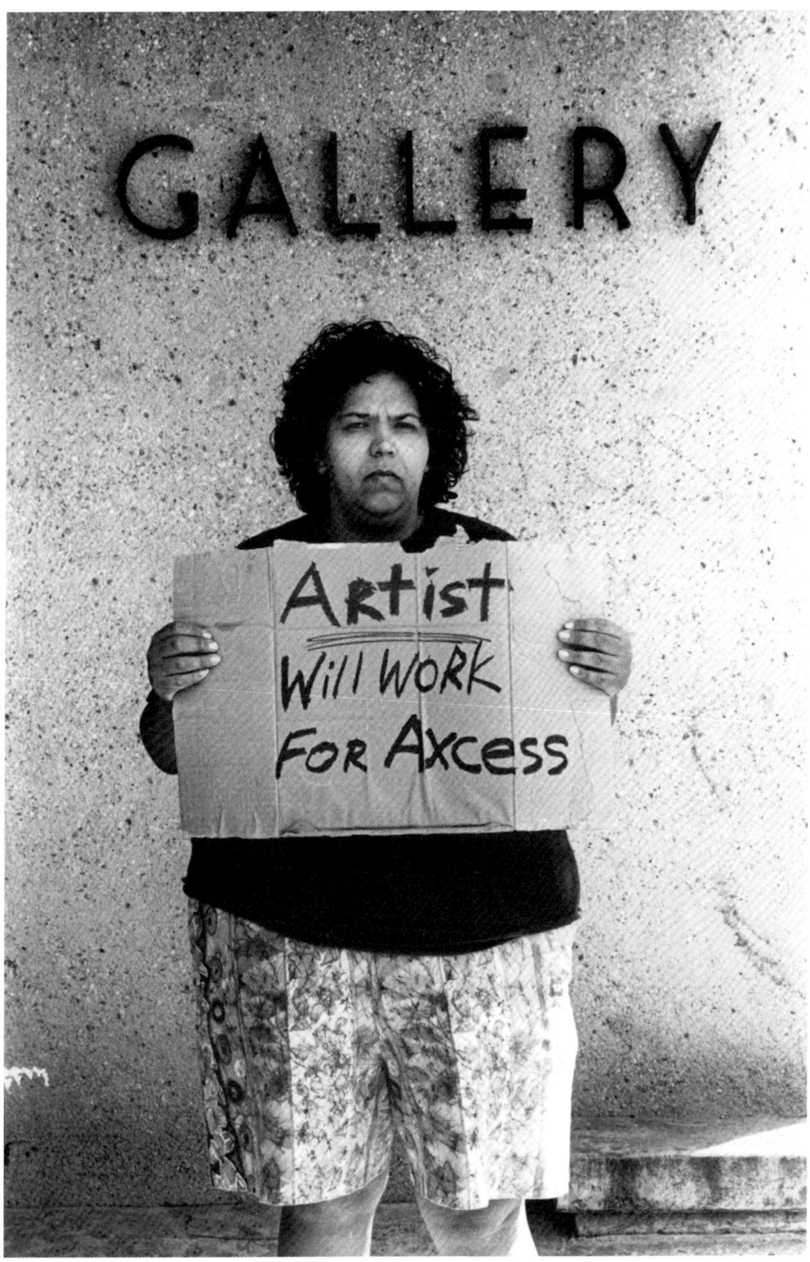

    Will Work For #4 1994

**DON'T TELL HER ART
CAN'T HURT**

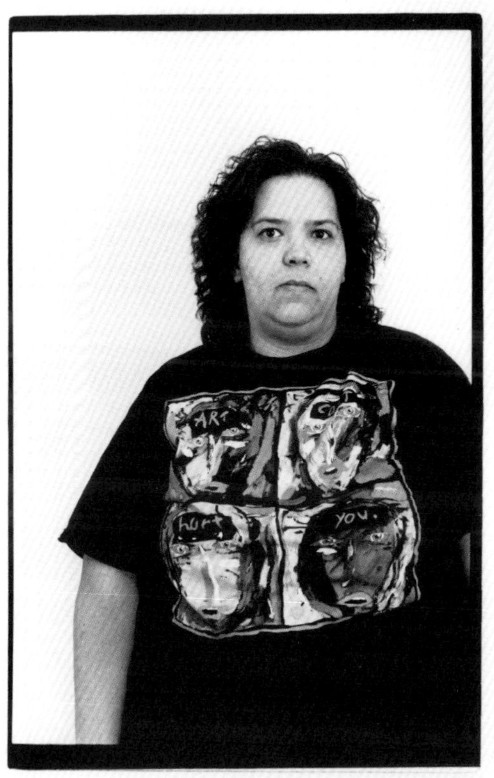

The t-shirt said ART can't hurt you, she
knew better. Her problem was she placed a
value on it. She believed in it just a
little too much she wanted to believe
that it was hers to have, to hold, and
to own.

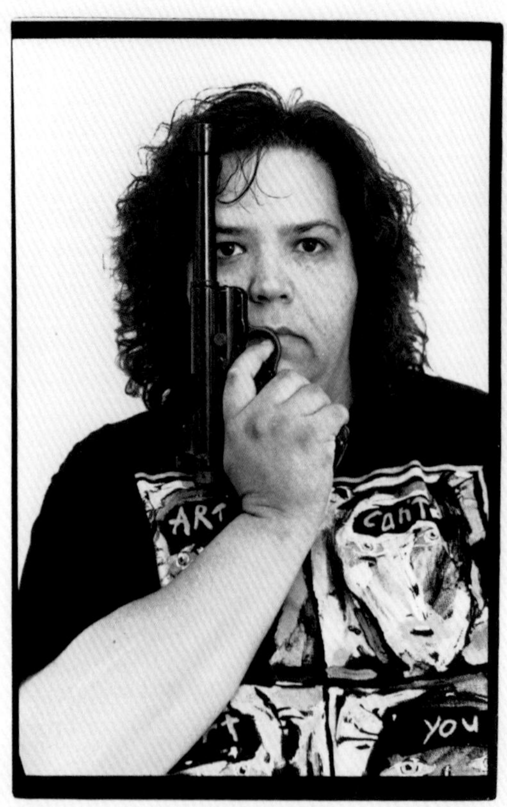

You learn you're not the one they want, talking about pride. It's the others who know about who we are. It's the others who want to teach us who we are.

 Don't Tell Her Art Can't Hurt (Part B) 1993

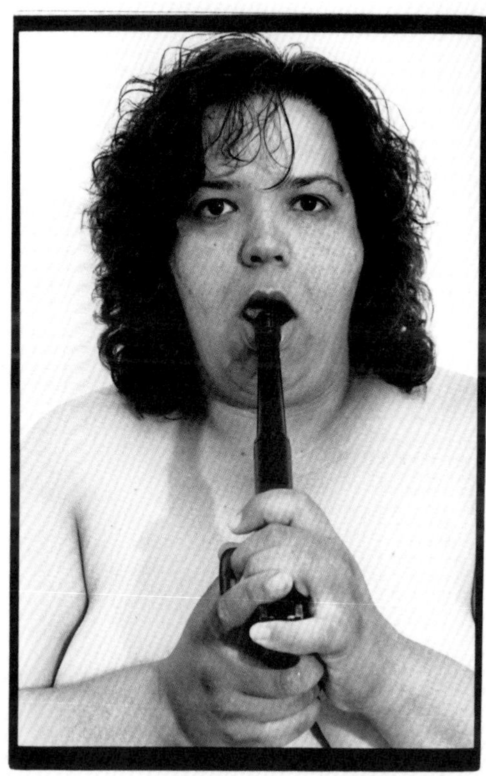

If you'RE A peRson of color and take pRide
in yourself and your CULtuRE, and you use
your ART to give A voice, to show the
positive, how do the bridges get built if
the doors are closed to your voice and
your vision?

   Don't Tell Her Art Can't Hurt (Part C) 1993

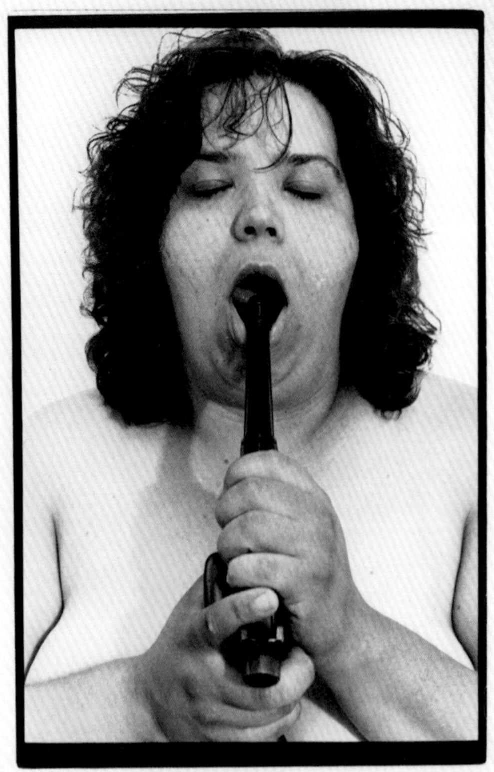

So don't tell her Art can't hurt, she
knows better. The believing can pull
At one's soul. So much that one
wants to give up.

    Don't Tell Her Art Can't Hurt (Part D) 1993

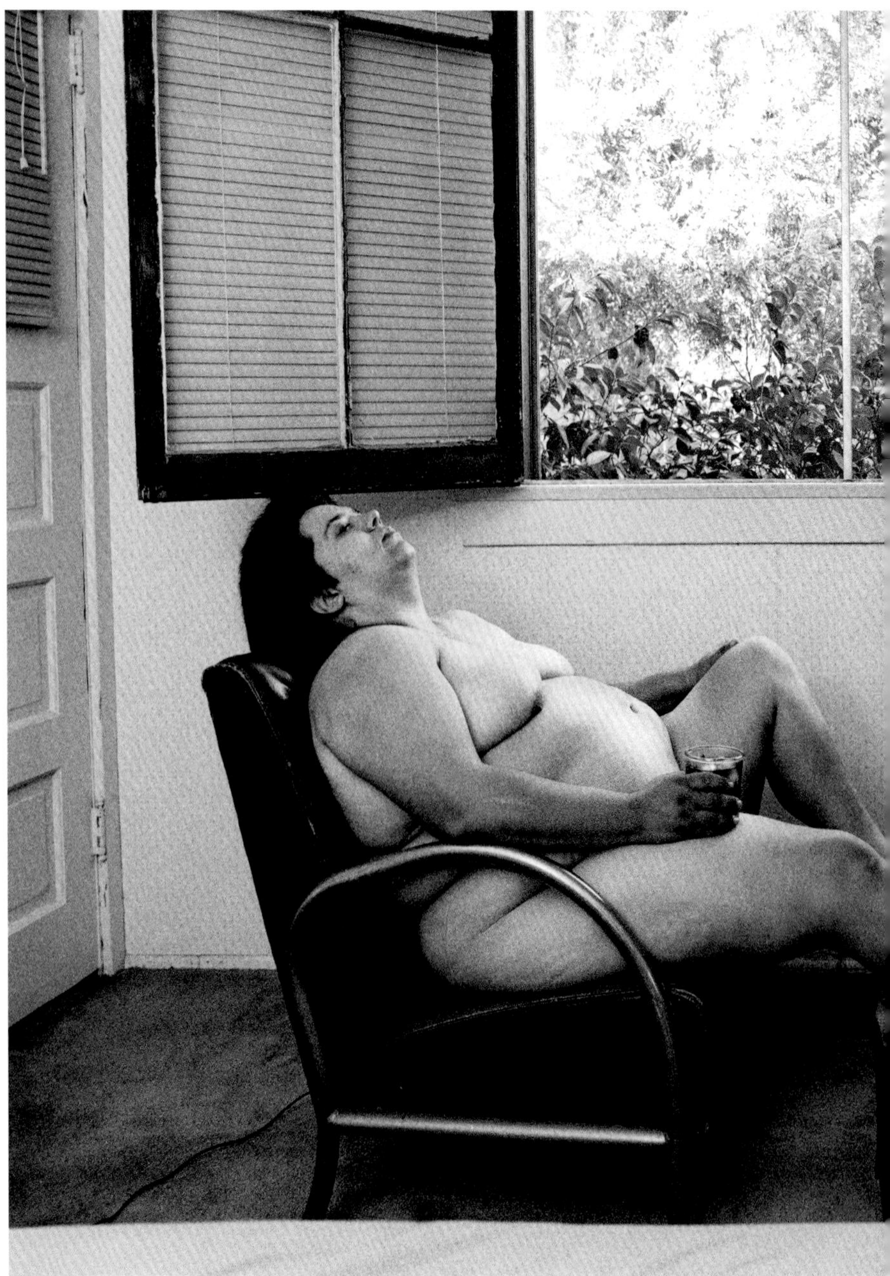

 In Sandy's Room 1989

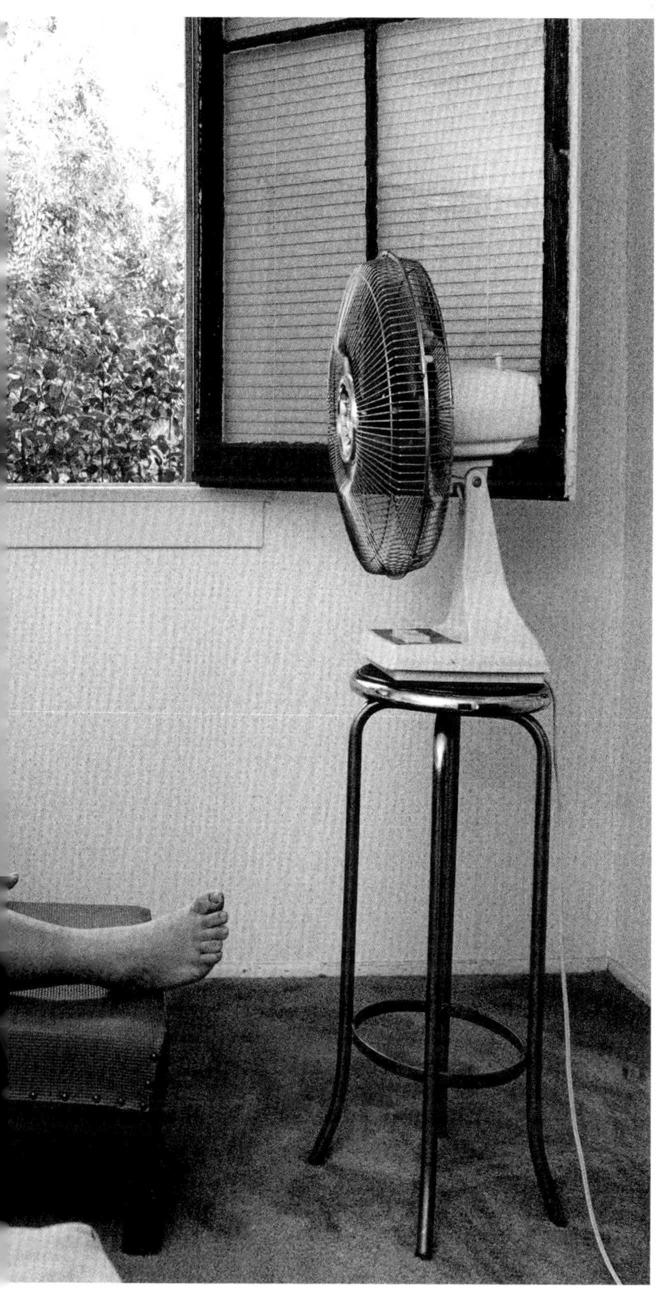

NATURE SELF-PORTRAIT

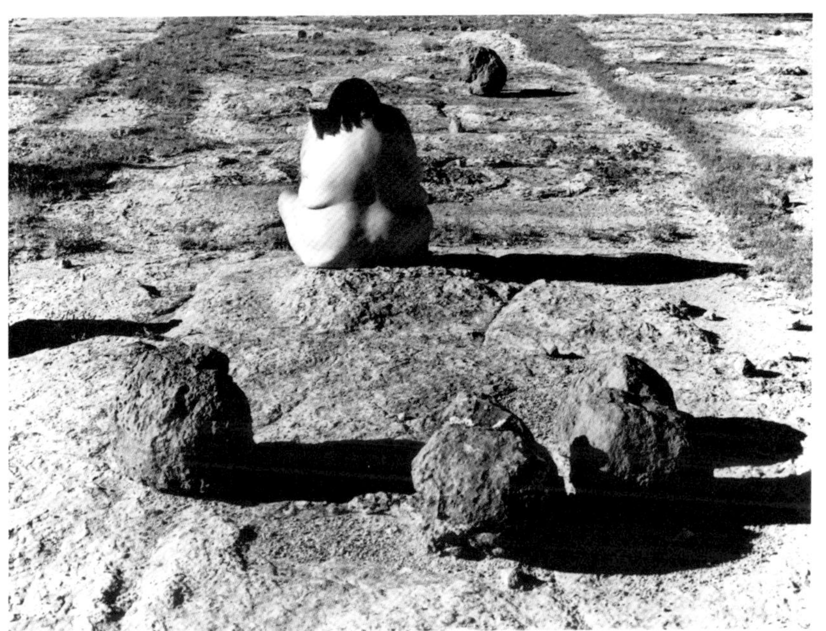

49   *Nature Self-Portrait #7 1996*

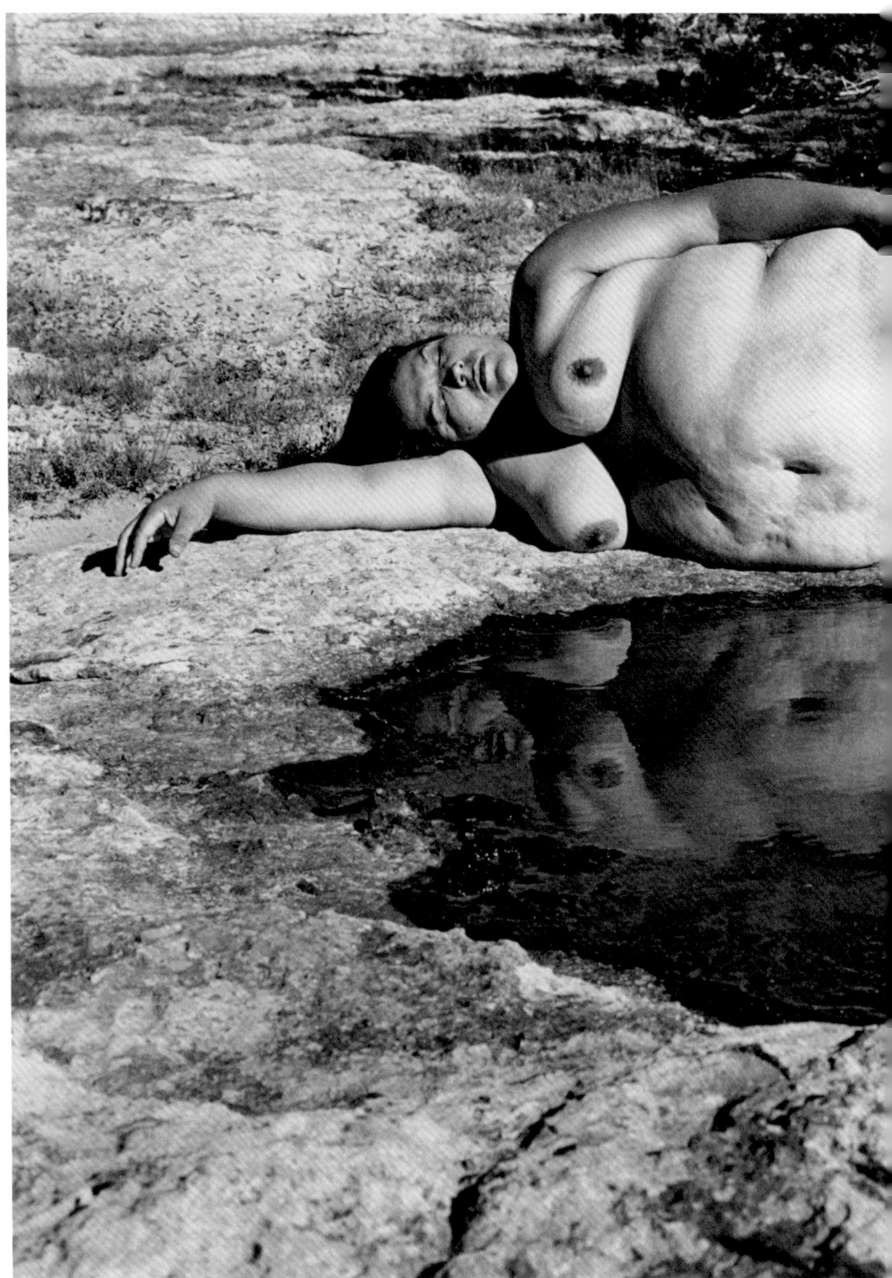

   Nature Self-Portrait #4 1996

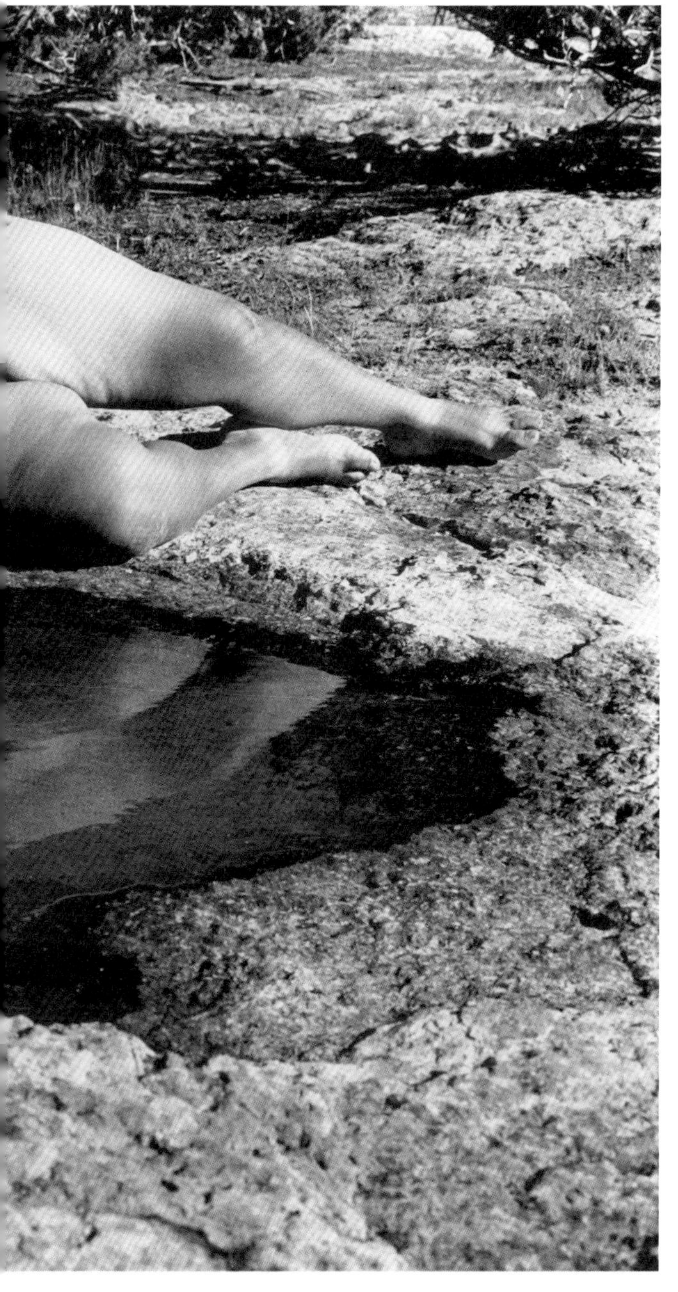

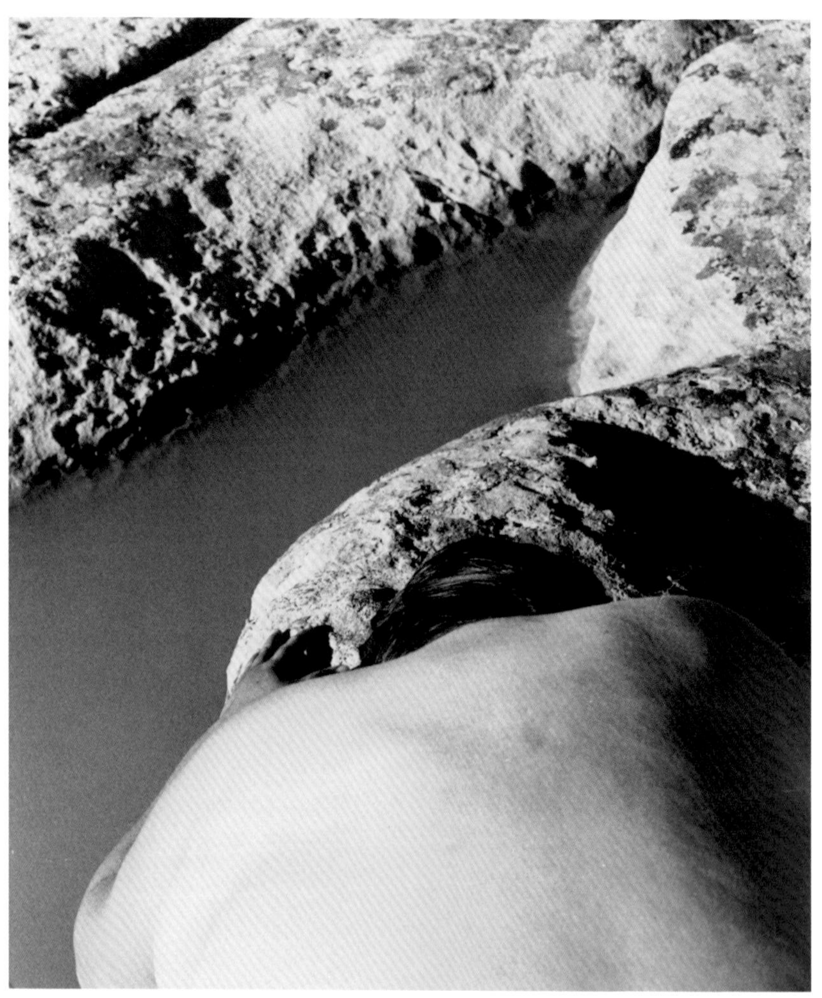

    Nature Self-Portrait #8 1996

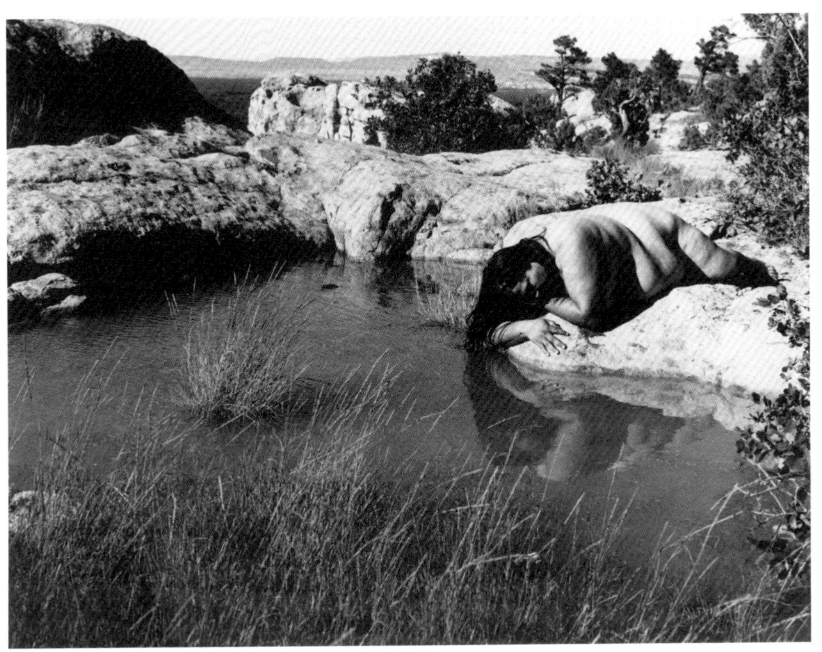

   Nature Self-Portrait #9 1996

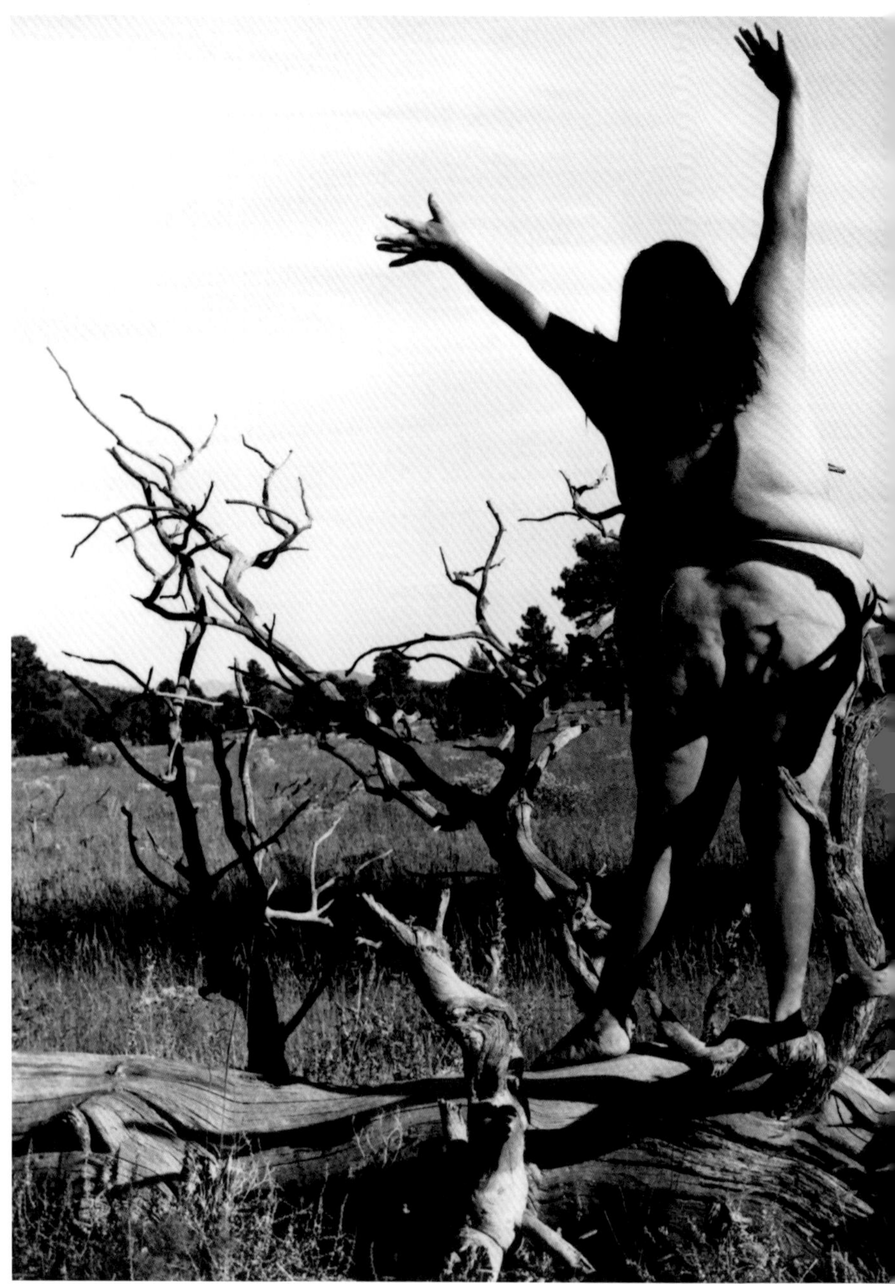

   Nature Self-Portrait #5 1996

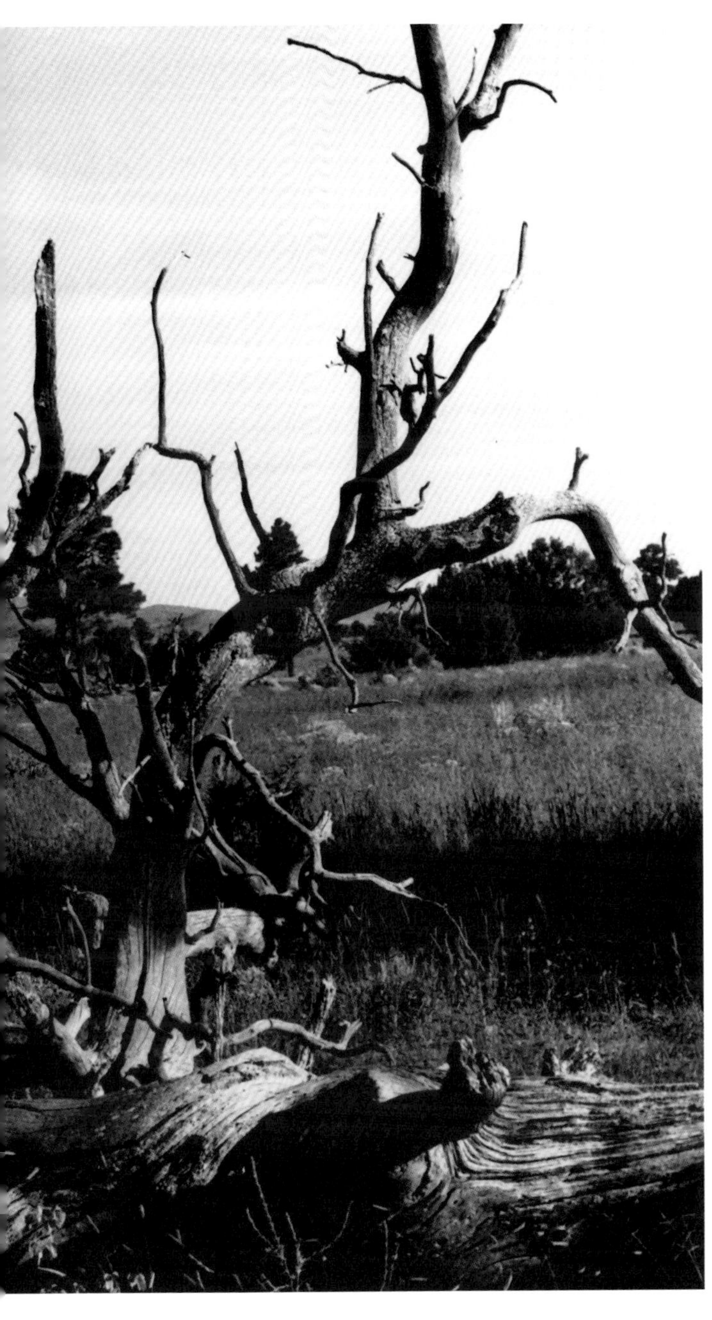

STILLNESS

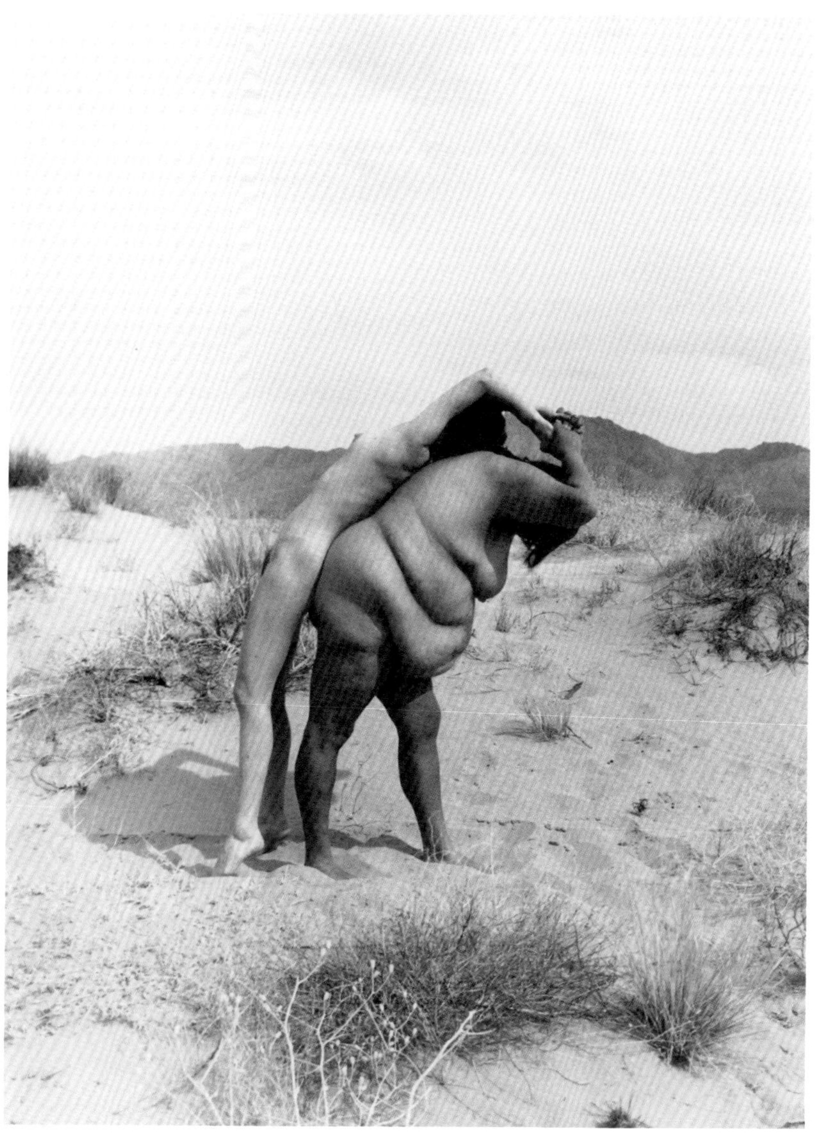

    Stillness #27 1999

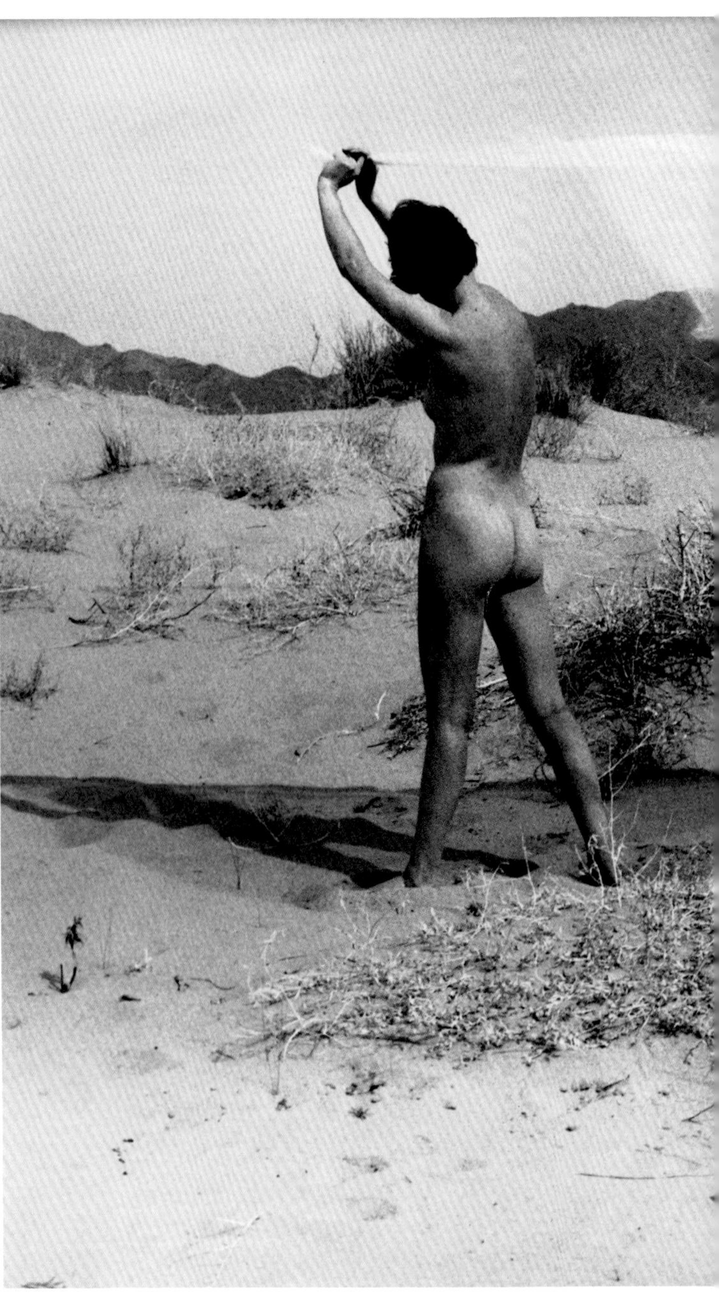

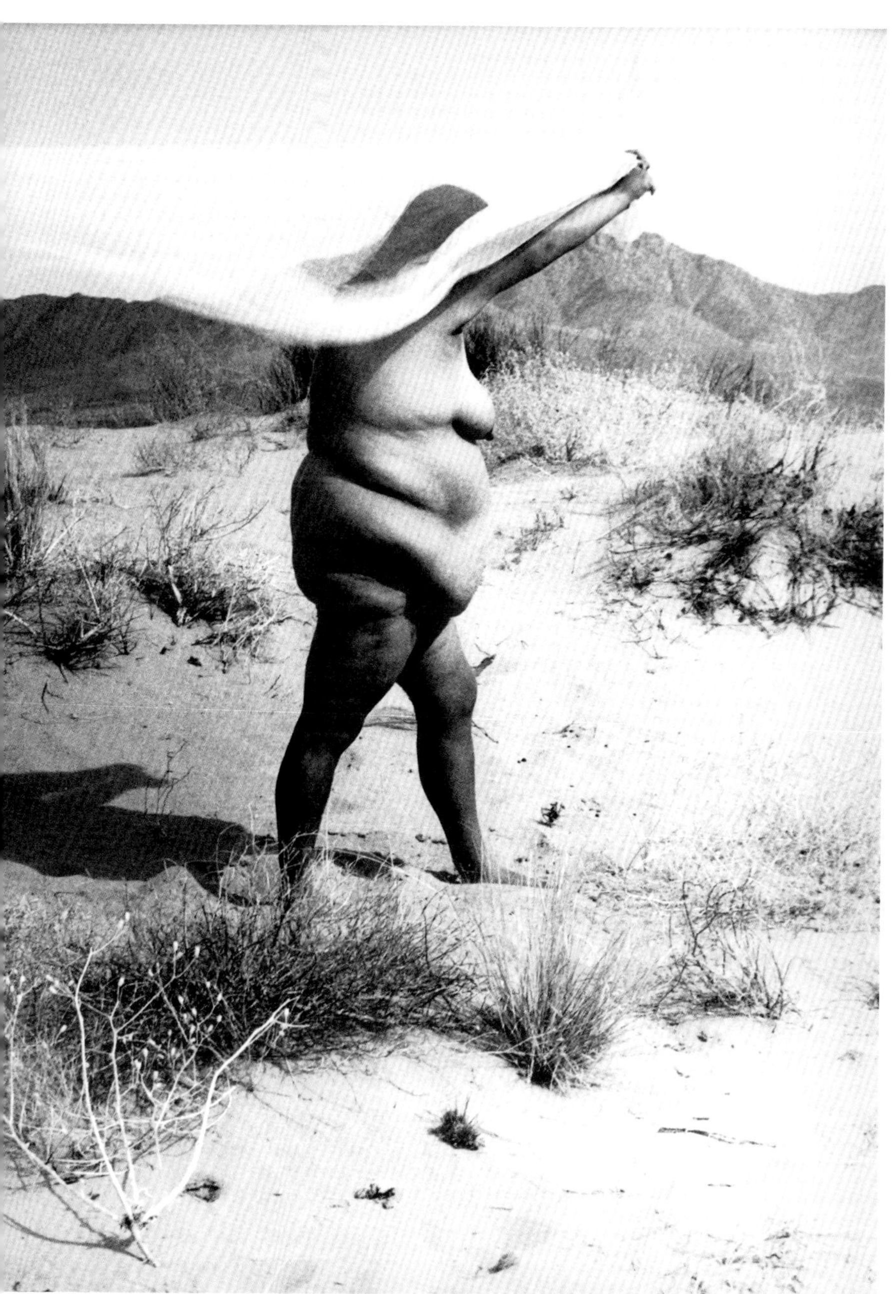

    Stillness #26 1999

MOTION

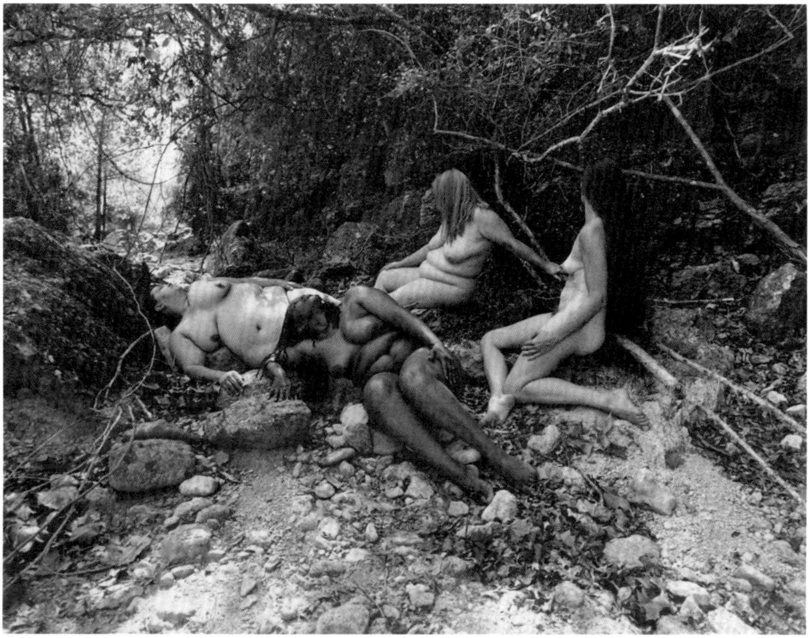

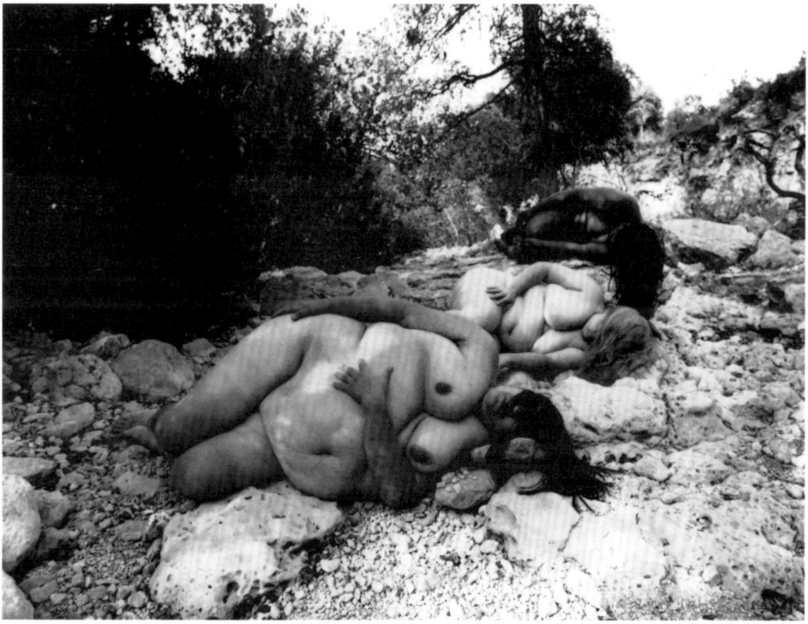

Motion #58 1999
Motion #56 1999

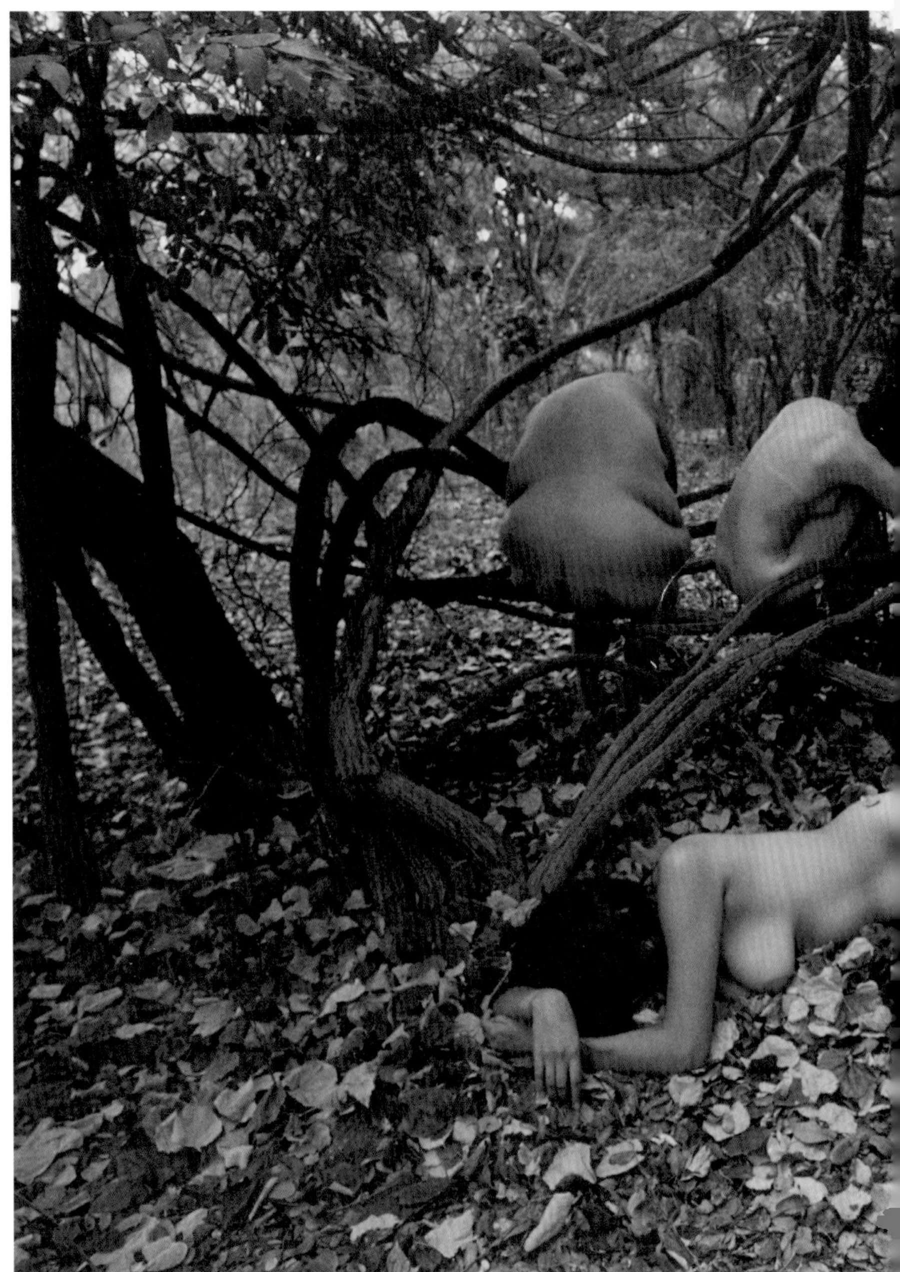

Motion #52 1999

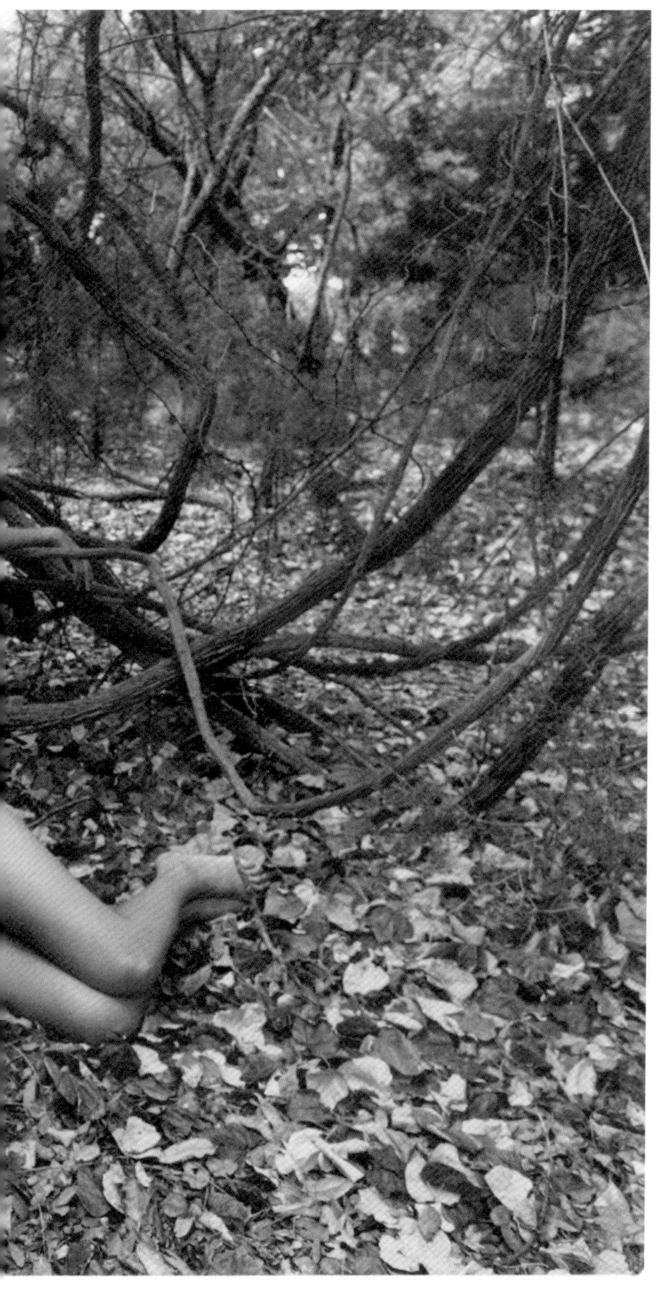

CREDITS

COPYRIGHT
All Images © Laura Aguilar Trust 2025

PHOTO CREDITS
Front cover, pp.31–7, pp.50–3, p.57, pp.61–3 Photo: Tate
All other photos: courtesy Laura Aguilar Trust

EDITOR'S ACKNOWLEDGEMENTS

Thank you to Laura Aguilar, whose images and words continue to inspire.

Special thanks to Christopher Velasco and Sybil Venegas, co-trustees of the Laura Aguilar Trust, for their help in the production of this book. And for their diligent and caring efforts to preserve and promote the work of the artist.

Thanks also to the Latin American Acquisition Committee and the Tate Americas Foundation, who were pivotal in supporting my curatorial efforts to bring Aguilar's work into the Tate collection.